Lux e Tenebris

FROM THE RARE AND ORIGINAL ALLEGORICAL PICTURE OF THE RELIGIONS OF THE WORLD, BY MOREAU, PARIS 1700

2021 Transactions of the Lux e Tenebris Chapter, Special Sankofa Edition

10 9 8 7 6 5 4 3 2 1

Cover Design by Jeffery Menzise, Ph.D. for Mind on the Matter Publishing

Library of Congress Cataloging-in-Publication Data
Lux e Tenebris,
Transactions of the Lux e Tenebris Chapter, Special Sankofa Edition includes Foreword, Cover Artwork, & Design by Jeff Menzise, Ph.D.

ISBN 979-8-9864121-0-8

Published in 2022 by
The Phylaxis Society
PO BOX 5675
Albuquerque, NM 87185-5675
Website: www.thephylaxis.org
Email: editor@thephylaxis.org

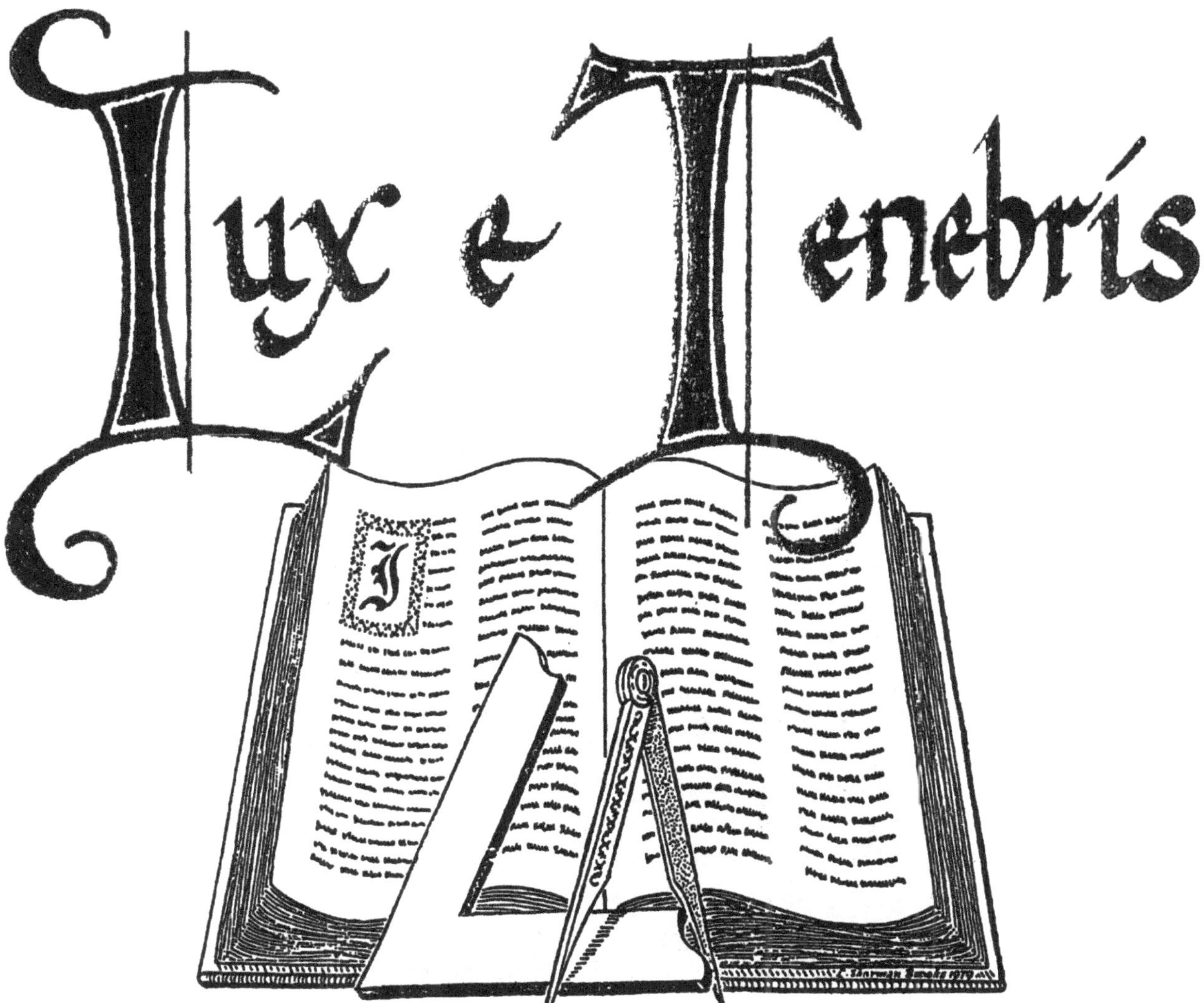

Lux e Tenebris

2021 Transactions
of the
Lux e Tenebris Chapter
of the
Phylaxis Society

Special Sankofa
Edition

Dedication

To Those Honorable Brothers Who Came Before Us,
Lighting the Path Forward That We Now Travel

ORIGIN AND PURPOSE OF THE PHYLAXIS SOCIETY

THE PHYLAXIS SOCIETY is an international organization of Prince Hall Freemasons who seek more light and who have light to impart. The Society provides a universal center and bond of union for Prince Hall Freemasons everywhere who desire to pursue the study of Prince Hall Masonry, receive light and disperse light. The Society will in no way interfere with the legislative and ritualistic affairs of any Masonic body.

The word PHYLAXIS is pronounced fi lak sis. Phyl is Greek for tribe, clan, race, and is akin to the Greek word phyein which means to bring forth — more to be. The PHYLAXIS means to guard and preserve. Symbolically we interpret it as to bring forth more light in Masonry, and to guard the Prince Hall Fraternity against its enemies. And to use the truth to preserve our Masonic heritage.

THE PHYLAXIS SOCIETY was designed to create a bond of union for Prince Hall Masonic writers and also to protect editors of Masonic publications from undeserved aggression by some "dressed in a little brief authority." It might be easy to pick on one isolated individual, but the prospect of being held up to the scorn of the whole Prince Hall Fraternity outside of one's own jurisdiction would give cause for pause.

The Society has become the leader in its field. To encourage Prince Hall Masonic study and endeavor to stimulate the writing of accurate and interesting Masonic articles for our own publication. In this manner it will foster the close, human relationship that is the ideal of Freemasonry.

Articles of Light

Editor's Note: Each Article is Presented with Much of Its Original Formatting, Therefore Paragraph Style, Sections, and Headers Will Vary from One Chapter to the Next.

Foreword

by Honorable Jeff Menzise, Ph.D., FPS (Life)

Tasked with producing the annual transactions of the Lux e Tenebris Chapter of The Phylaxis Society, I was faced with the pressure of what seemed to be an insurmountable obstacle: making this happen without a pool of current articles. In an ideal world, the transactions are published from a selection of many manuscripts submitted by the current membership; in 2021, this was not the case.

Due to health reasons, Covid-related adjustments, professional obligations & duties, or simply not following through on one's stated commitment, this year's selection of potential articles was slim to none. As we all know, pressure bursts pipes; but it also creates diamonds...it all depends on how the material responds to said pressure. Fortunately, we, as Prince Hall Masons, are in the diamond mining business; we come pressure-tested, and are built to produce brilliance under pressure.

One day, while meditating on how to go about generating the 2021 Transactions, our Ancestors whispered in my ear, "We are hear to serve." Initially, I was confused by this cryptic message, not fully understanding that these words were in reference to the 2021 Transactions. About 8 months prior to receiving this message, I reached out to several Elders within the Phylaxis Society, in search of past issues of the Lux e Tenebris Transactions, for the sole purpose of seeing what had been produced in the past, and hopefully learning from their wisdom and research efforts. I had forgotten that a few years prior to that, Honorable Brother Tommy Rigmaiden, FPS (Life), sent me a copy of the 2013 Transactions, which he assembled while serving as both Director and Master of the Lux e Tenebris Chapter. I could add to this treasure trove of Masonic scholarship, the three (3) editions sent to me by Honorable Brother Rev. Dr. Robert Uzzel, Jr., FPS, complete with his thoughts, rebuttals, and further references and insights etched in his pen throughout. I emerged from this meditation realizing I had exactly what is needed to produce a series of Lux e Tenebris transactions honoring those who came before us, by resurrecting their voices and contributions in what I am calling, *The Special Sankofa Edition*.

These volumes will consist of the best and most intriguing of articles previously published in the Transactions of the Lux e Tenebris Research Chapter. Unfortunately, the record in my possession is incomplete, and only spans a few non-consecutive years; however, we are fortunate that each article is dense, of good quality, and, full of insight, wisdom, facts, research references, and even statements encouraging future generations of Lux e Tenebris and Phylaxis members, to expand upon these articles, knowing that new information would be unearthed over the next four decades.

In this current edition, you will find articles from Honorable Brothers Joseph Walkes, Robert Uzzel, Herman Slaughter, Floyd Bass, and Tommy Rigmaiden. Each author writing for the purpose of advancing our understanding and comprehension of some aspect of Freemasonry in general, and more specifically, to those descending from African Lodge. We are fortunate to still have Brothers Rigmaiden and Uzzel alive and active in our Fraternity at the time of this publication. Let's give these two Brothers their flowers while they can still enjoy the smell.

In our African traditions, we are taught to live a life that is upright, and one that makes beneficial contributions to humanity, for the sake of future generations. Successfully living such a lifestyle, would guarantee that your name is remembered for generations to come; long after the last grain of sand falls in your hour glass. Each Brother featured in this volume, has lived a life and/or made contributions to the Craft, which should guarantee that their names become permanently etched into the records of Prince Hall Freemasonry.

Much like the Ancient Builders honored in our Modern rituals, I have taken the stones of older and previous temples, in order to erect this current edifice. The stones have been carefully selected according to their ability to reflect and produce Light for our current reader. These smooth stones have retained their intrinsic value, and therefore, are deemed worthy of a place in this new structure. This is why the current transactions bear the name, "Sankofa."

Among the Akan culture in Ghana, West Africa, Sankofa is the name given to one of the many Adinkra symbols. These sacred symbols are used to efficiently and effectively convey complex and moral messages to live by; a sort of blueprint for social harmony. According to Adinkra scholar and author, W. Bruce Willis:

> Even though adinkra has been defined as 'the intelligence or message that each soul takes with him from God upon obtaining leave to depart to earth,' these messages can be extremely beneficial to the living as a model of good and respectful living.
>
> Adinkra symbols are figurative and stylized geometric images that embody the legendary history of the Akan people and their cultural truths. Each symbol em-

> bodies poetic messages, proverbs, and maxims about Nature, the universe, and the myths, beliefs, rituals and philosophy of the people.
>
> The symbols have the potential to be interpreted on various levels. Coming out of an oral society, there is a great deal of philosophical material embedded in the proverbs, myths and traditions of the people...To be able to understand the symbols, one has to literally undergo somewhat of a cultural apprenticeship, because all of the symbols may be interpreted in different ways or they have a variety of meanings.

The Sankofa symbol, according to Arthur, as cited by Willis,

> is based on a mythical bird...(and) reflects the Akan belief that the past serves as a guide for planning the future, or the wisdom in learning from the past in building the future. The Akan believe that there must be movement with times but as the forward march proceeds, the gems must be picked from behind and carried forward on the march.

It is my prayer that this series brings honor to those whose works I have reproduced; and that I have done them justice whenever I have edited for grammer or spelling, or altered the layout for the sake of readability. In most instances, I have preserved the original condition and presentation. In the spirit of Sankofa, let us all seek to "Fetch from our Past, In Order to Produce a Vibrant Future," by mining the gems published herein.

Honorable Jeff Menzise, Ph.D., FPS (Life)
Director, Lux e Tenebris Research Chapter

Dissecting the Landmarks

by Honorable Herman L. Slaughter, MPS

(1st Edition, 1983-84)

According to Webster's Dictionary, a landmark is a "conspicuous object serving to bound or identify a place."

Albert G. Mackey, noted Masonic authority, admits in his statement about Landmarks, "The first requisite therefore, of a custom or rule of action to constitute a Landmark is that it must have existed from time whereof the memory of man runneth not to the contrary." They are sufficiently numerous to act as bulwarks against innovations, but not sufficient to stand in the way of needful reform.

Albert Bede, author of "Landmarks of Freemasonry," says:

> We are wholly dependent for a definition of Landmarks on recognized Masonic authorities, and each of these declares for himself what he believes is the correct definition. Any Masonic student may do the same with exactly the same likelihood that his definition will gain world wide recognition.

After thirty years and some Masonic study and research, I am attempting to dissect the Landmarks as listed by Bro. Albert G. Mackey and to point out the ancient usages of customs which I deem to be Landmarks.

The Landmarks of Freemasonry have long been a controversial subject among those brave souls who have had courage enough to express their opinions concerning these all important Landmarks.

First, can we determine what the Landmarks are? No Grand Lodge, to my knowledge, has ever attempted to enumerate the Ancient Landmarks. The Premiere Grand Lodge of the World, or the United Grand Lodge of England, has never given a definition or published an enumeration.

Of course, we can never have a world-wide accepted definition because there is no world-wide organization of Freemasons with power to promulgate a definition.

To quote some of the authorities:

George Oliver says,

some restrict the Landmarks to the Obligation, signs, tokens, and words; others include the ceremonies of initiation, passing and raising; and the forms dimensions and supports; the ground situation and covering; the ornaments, furniture and jewels of a Lodge, or their characteristic symbols; some think the Order has no Landmarks beyond its peculiar secrets.

Author's note: Oliver does not commit himself as to his own beliefs.

Robert Morris says,

The Landmarks are 'the fixed tenets by which the limits of Freemasonry may be known' and preserved.

Joseph H. Drummond says,

The only evidence that some customs are Landmarks is the fact that they are mentioned as such in the earliest publications in relation to Freemasonry.

Hexstall says,

The Landmarks of English Freemasonry are those fundamental grand principles of our peculiar system of morality which were adopted by the founders of the Premier Grand Lodge as essentials, or which have been declared by competent authority to be Landmarks.

Gould, famed as a Masonic Historian, says,

Of Ancient Landmarks it may be said with more or less foundation of truth; nobody knows what they comprise or omit, there are no earthly authority because everything is a Landmark when an opponent desires to silence you, but nothing is a Landmark that stands in his own way.

Albert Pike says,

The fundamental principles of Ancient Operatives were few and simple and they were not called Landmarks.

Thomas S. Ray, P.G.M. of Massachusetts says,

A Landmark is one of the boundary marks by which Freemasonry is enclosed and our use of Landmarks indicate that Freemasonry is interested in boundaries.

Dr. Mackey whose definitions of Landmarks are the most popular among Freemasons today says,

Perhaps the safest method is to restrict them to those Ancient and therefore universal customs of the Order which either gradually grew into operation as rules of action or once enacted by any competent authority were enacted at a period so remote that no record of their origin is to be found in the records of history.

Both the enactors and the time of their enactment have passed away from the record and the Landmarks are therefore of higher antiquity than memory or history can read.

Dr. Mackey's list, being the most popular, we will examine them.

LANDMARK No. 1

THE MODE OF RECOGNITION —

The Obligations, signs, tokens and words are agreed by all Masonic authorities to be a Landmark. They admit of no variation and if they have suffered alteration or addition, the evil of such a violation of the ancient law has always made itself subsequently manifest. An admission of this is to be found in the proceedings of the Masonic Congress at Paris, where a proposal was presented to render these modes of recognition once more universal — a proposition which never would have been necessary if the integrity of this important Landmark had been rigorously preserved.

COMMENT — See Comment Under Landmark No. 2

LANDMARK No. 2

THE DIVISION OF SYMBOLIC MASONRY INTO THREE DEGREES —

Is a Landmark that has been better preserved than any other, although even here the mischievous spirit of innovation has left its traces and by the disruption of its concluding portion from the third degree, a wealth of information has been created in respect to the final teaching of the Master's Order and the Royal Arch of England, Scotland, Ireland and America and the "High Degrees of France and Germany are all made to differ in the mode in which they lead the Neophyte to the great consummation of all symbolic Masonry. In 1813, the Grand Lodge of England vindicated the Ancient Landmarks, by solemnly enacting that Ancient Craft Masonry consisted of the three Degrees of Entered Apprentice, Fellowcraft and Master Mason, including the Holy Royal Arch. But the disruption has never been healed, and the Landmark, although acknowledged in its integrity by all, still continues to be violated.

COMMENT — H.L. Haywood, in his "Story of Freemasonry," states that in 1717, the Old Bodies of Ceremonies, Customs, Rules and Symbols which had formed about Apprentices and Fellow, had become crystallized into what are now called degrees. The evidence indicates Landmarks 1 and 2 as true Landmarks. Landmark No. 2 was established as a Landmark after 1725. The entire contents of the three degrees had previously been contained in two degrees.

LANDMARK No. 3

THE LEGEND OF THE THIRD DEGREE

...an important Landmark, the integrity of which has been well preserved. There is no rite of Masonry practiced in any country or language in which the essential elements of this legend are not taught. The lectures may vary and indeed are constantly changing. But the legend has ever remained the same and it is necessary that it should be so. For the legend of the Temple Builder constitutes the very essence and identity of Masonry. Any rite which should exclude it or materially alter it would at once, by that exclusion or alteration, cease to be a Masonic rite.

COMMENT — "The Drama of Faith" has always been a part of Freemasonry. Whether it be the Hiramic Legend or The Legend of Isis and Osiris or Adonis as in Adoniac or Syrian Mysteries.

LANDMARK No. 4

THE GOVERNMENT OF THE FRATERNITY

...by a presiding Officer called a Grand Master, who is elected from the body of the Craft. It is a fourth Landmark of the Order. Many persons ignorantly suppose that the election of the Grand Master is held in consequence of a law or regulation of the Grand Lodge. Such however is not the case. The office is indebted for its existence to a Landmark of the institution long before Grand Lodges were established. If the present system of the legislative government by Grand Lodges were to be abolished, a Grand Master would still be necessary. Although there has been a period within the records of history when a Grand Lodge was unknown, there never has been a time when the Craft did not have their Grand Master.

COMMENT — Only a portion of the above Landmark is true. There have always been Grand Masters, but the Grand Master was not always elected from the body of the Craft. The Grand Master prior to 1717 were commissioned by the King of England.

LANDMARK No. 5

THE PREROGATIVE OF THE GRAND MASTER TO PRESIDE

...over every assembly of the Craft, wherever and whensoever held, is a fifth Landmark. It is in consequence of this law, derived from ancient usage and not from any special enactment, that the Grand Master assumes the chair or as it is called in England "The Throne" at every communication of the Grand Lodge and that of every subordinate Lodge where he may happen to be present.

COMMENT — This Landmark is superfluous and is covered by Landmark No. 4.

LANDMARK No. 6

THE PREROGATIVE OF THE GRAND MASTER TO GRANT DISPENSATIONS

...for conferring degrees at irregular times is another and a very important Landmark. The statutory law of Masonry requires a month or other determinate period to elapse between the presentation of a petition and the election of a candidate. But the Grand Master has the power to set aside or dispense with this probation, as no statute can impair his prerogative he still retains the law although the Masters of Lodges no longer possess it.

LANDMARK No. 7

THE PREROGATIVE OF THE GRAND MASTER TO GIVE DISPENSATIONS FOR OPENING AND HOLDING LODGES

...is another Landmark. He must grant in virtue of this, to sufficient number of Masons, the privilege of meeting together and conferring degrees. The Lodges thus established are called "Lodges Under Dispensation." They are strictly creatures of the Grand Master, created by his authority, existing only during his will and pleasure, and liable at any moment to be dissolved at his command. They may be continued for a day, a month or six months, but whatever be the period of their existence, they are indebted for that existence only to the grace of the Grand Master.

COMMENT — Landmark No. 7 is covered by No. 6

Landmark No. 8

THE PREROGATIVE OF THE GRAND MASTER TO MAKE MASONS AT SIGHT

...is a Landmark which is closely connected with the preceding one. There has been misapprehension in relation to this Landmark which misapprehension led to a denial of its existence in jurisdictions where the Grand Master was perhaps at the very time substantially expressing the prerogative, without the slightest remark or opposition. It is not to be supposed that the Grand Master can retire with a profane end to a private room and there, without assistance, confer the degrees of Freemasonry upon him. No such prerogative exists, and yet many believe that this is the so much talked of right of "making Masons at sight."

The real mode and the only mode of exercising the prerogative is this. The Grand Master summons to his assistance not less than six other Masons, convenes a Lodge and without any previous probation, but on sight of the candidate, confers the degrees upon him, after which he dissolves the Lodge, and dismisses the brethren.

Lodges thus convened for special purposes are called occasional Lodges. This is the only way in which any Grand Master within the records of the institution has ever been known to "Make Masons at Sight." The prerogative is dependent upon that of granting dispensations to open and hold Lodges. If the Grand Master has power of granting to any other Mason the privilege of presiding over Lodges working by his dispensation, he may assume this privilege of presiding himself, and as no one can deny his right to grant to a number of brethren at a distance, and to dissolve the Lodge at his pleasure and will.

The making of Masons at sight is only the conferring of degrees by the Grand

Master, at once, in an occasional Lodge, constituted by his dispensing power for the purpose and over which he presides in person.

COMMENT — I consider this to be an ancient Landmark which without the fraternity would lose one of its spectacular features which set it apart as with Landmark No. 6 and No. 7.

Landmark No. 9

THE NECESSITY FOR MASONS TO CONGREGATE IN LODGES

It is not to be misunderstood by this that any ancient Landmark has directed that permanent organization of subordinate Lodges which constitute one of the features of the Masonic system as it prevails now. But the Landmarks of the Order always prescribed that Masons should, from time to time, congregate themselves together for the purpose of either operative or speculative labor and that these congregations should be called Lodges.

Formerly these were temporary meetings called together for special purposes and then dissolved; the brethren parting to meet again at other times and other places according to the necessity of circumstances. But warrants of constitution, bylaws, permanent officers and annual arrears are modern innovations wholly outside of the Landmarks and dependent entirely on the special enactments of a comparatively recent period.

COMMENT — This was never a Landmark, but was the results of the occasion of laboring in their trade.

Landmark No. 10

THE GOVERNMENT OF THE CRAFT

...when so congregated in a Lodge by a Master and two Wardens, is also a Landmark. To show the influence of this ancient law, it may be observed that a congregation of Masons meeting together under any other government, as that for instance of President and Vice President, or Chairman and Sub-chairman, would not be recognized as a Lodge. The presence of a Master and two Wardens is as essential to the valid organization of a Lodge as a warrant of Constitution in different languages, the Master for instance being called "Venerable" in French Masonry and the Wardens "Surveillants," but the officers, their number, prerogatives and duties are everywhere identical.

COMMENT — The governing of a Masonic Lodge by a Master and two Wardens or by whatever name they may be called is essential for the preservation of the character of Freemasonry.

Landmark No. 11

THE NECESSITY THAT EVERY LODGE WHEN CONGREGATED SHOULD BE DULY TYLED

...is an important Landmark of the institution which is never neglected. The necessity of this law arises from the esoteric character of Masonry. As a secret institution, its portals must be guarded from intrusion of the profane. Such a law must therefore always have been in force from the very beginning of the Order. It is therefore properly classed among the most ancient Landmarks. The office of Tyler is wholly independent of any special enactment of Grand or subordinate Lodges, although these may and do prescribe for him additional duties which vary in different jurisdictions. But the duty of guarding the door, and keeping off cowans and eavesdroppers is an ancient one which constitutes a Landmark for his government.

COMMENT — This is a Landmark that has come down to us from a time no one has a recollection or record of, and is necessary for the retaining of the secrecy or privacy of our Order.

Landmark No. 12

THE RIGHT OF EVERY MASON TO BE REPRESENTED

...in all general meetings of the craft and to instruct his representatives, is a twelfth Landmark. Formerly, these general meetings, which were usually held once a year, were called "General Assemblies," and all the fraternity, even to the youngest Entered Apprentice, were permitted to be present. Now they are called "Grand Lodges," and only the Masters and Wardens of the Subordinate Lodges are summoned. But this is simply as the representatives of their members. Originally, each Mason represented himself; now he is represented by his officers. This was a concession granted by the fraternity about 1717, and of course does not affect the integrity of the Landmark, for the principle of representation is still preserved. The concession was only made for purposes of convenience.

COMMENT — This is not a Landmark. Today, General Meetings are called Grand Lodges. Formerly they were called General Assemblies, and every Master Mason was summoned to attend. It was not a right, but an obligation. Today, the Master Mason has the right to be represented by his Master and/or his Wardens. This came about in 1717 and was merely for the convenience of the Brethren.

Landmark No. 13

THE RIGHT OF EVERY MASON TO APPEAL

... from the decision of his brethren in Lodge convened, to the Grand Lodge or General Assembly of Masons, is a Landmark highly essential to the preservation of justice, and the prevention of oppression. A few modern Grand Lodges, in adopting a regulation that the decision of Subordinate Lodges, in cases of expulsion, cannot be wholly set aside upon an appeal, have violated this unquestioned Landmark, as well as the principles of just government.

COMMENT — I am in accord with this as being a Landmark. To take away a Mason's right to appeal would destroy the fabric of Freemasonry as we are admonished to reprehend with justice.

Landmark No. 14

THE RIGHT OF EVERY MASON TO VISIT

... and sit in every regular Lodge is an unquestionable Landmark of the Order. This is called "the right of visitation." This right of visitation has always been recognized as an inherent right, which inures to every Mason as he travels through the world. And this is because Lodges are justly considered as only divisions for convenience of the universal Masonic family. This right may, of course be impaired or forfeited on special occasions by various circumstances; but when admission is refused to a Mason in good standing, who knocks at the door of a Lodge as a visitor, it is to be expected that some good and sufficient reason shall be furnished for this violation, of what is in general a Masonic right, founded on the Landmarks of the Order.

Landmark No. 15

THE EXAMINATION OF UNKNOWN BRETHREN

No brother, unknown to members present, can be admitted into a Lodge without first passing an examination according to ancient usage. Of course, if the visitor is known to any brother present to be a Mason in good standing and if that brother will vouch for his qualifications, the examination may be dispensed with, as the Landmark refers, only to the cases of strangers who are to be recognized unless after strict trial, due examination, or lawful information.

COMMENT — Mackey's 15th Landmark could be incorporated into the 14th Landmark.

Landmark No. 16

NO LODGE CAN INTERFERE IN THE BUSINESS OF ANOTHER LODGE

...nor give degrees to brethren who are members of another or other Lodges. This undoubtedly is an ancient Landmark, founded on the great principle of courtesy of our institution. It has been repeatedly recognized by subsequent statutory enactments of all Grand Lodges.

COMMENT — We have had many disputes as to jurisdiction over candidates, and many Lodges have acted to stop work being conferred on candidates elected in other Lodges. In some jurisdictions, members of one Lodge may vote on petitions in other Lodges, as stated in Landmark 14. Lodges are considered as only divisions for convenience.

Ancient usage and custom did not allow for the separation of the brethren. This custom became law after the conversion from operative to speculative.

Landmark No. 17

EVERY FREEMASON IS AMENABLE TO THE LAWS AND REGULATIONS OF THE JURISDICTION OF HIS RESIDENCE

Although he may not be a member of any Lodge (which is in fact itself a Masonic offense — non-affiliation). It does not exempt a Mason from Masonic jurisdiction.

COMMENT — Thus a point for the universality of Freemasonry.

Landmark No. 18

QUALIFICATIONS OF CANDIDATES FOR INITIATION

...are derived from a Landmark of the Order. These qualifications are, that he shall be a man, shall be unmutilated, freeborn and of mature age. That is to say, a woman, a cripple, a slave, or one born in slavery is disqualified for initiation into the rites of Masonry. Statutes, it is true, have from time to time been enacted, enforcing or explaining these principles, but the qualifications really arise from the very nature of the Masonic institution, and from its symbolic teachings and have always existed as Landmarks.

COMMENT — As we study these Landmarks, let us keep in mind Dr. Mackey's statement about the Landmarks,

> The first requisite therefore, of a custom or rule of action to constitute a Landmark is, that it must have existed from a time whereof the memory of man runneth not to the contrary.
>
> They are sufficiently numerous to act as bulwarks against innovations, but not sufficient to stand in the way of needful reform.

The very nature of our institutions disqualified No. 18 as a Landmark. Although understandable reasons are given in Mackey's footnotes, for not qualifying a slave for membership there is no unbiased reason for not qualifying a free man, one who was born in slavery, but acquired his freedom later (as slave or a bondsman cannot freely follow the dictates of his mind. He is not his own man). Here is a case of needful reform, so No. 18 is eliminated as a Landmark. Masonry regards no man for his status or station in life.

Landmark No. 19

A BELIEF IN THE EXISTENCE OF GOD AS THE GRAND ARCHITECT OF THE UNIVERSE

...is one of the most important Landmarks of the Order. It has been always deemed essential that a denial of the existence of a Supreme and superintending power is an absolute disqualification for initiation. The annals of the Order never yet have furnished an instance in which an avowed atheist was ever made a Mason. The very initiatory ceremonies of the first degree forbid and prevent the possibility of so monstrous an occurrence.

COMMENT — This is an unquestionable Landmark, for the Old Charges say, "A Mason is obliged by his tenure to obey the moral law and if he rightfully understands the art, he will never be a stupid atheist nor an irreligious libertine."

Landmark No. 20

THE BELIEF IN A RESURRECTION TO A FUTURE LIFE

This Landmark is not so positively impressed on the candidate by exact words as the preceding but the doctrine is taught by very plain implication and runs through the whole symbolism of the Order.

To believe in Masonry and not to believe in a resurrection would be an absurd anomaly, which should only be excused by the reflection that he who thus confounded his belief and his skepticism, was so ignorant of the meaning of both theories as to have no rational foundation for his knowledge of either.

COMMENT — One needs only to reflect on the "Drama of Faith" (in our case, The Legend of the Temple Builder, or the Hiramic Legend) to know that this is a Landmark.

Landmark No. 21

A BOOK OF THE LAW SHALL CONSTITUTE AN INDISPENSABLE PART OF THE FURNITURE OF EVERY LODGE.

I say advisedly, a "Book of the Law," because it is not absolutely required that everywhere the Old Testament and the New Testament shall be used. The Book of the Law is that volume, which by the religion of the country, is believed to contain the revealed Will of the Grand Architect of the Universe. Hence, in all Lodges of Christian countries, the Book of the Law is composed of the Old and New Testaments; in a country where Judaism was the prevailing faith, the Old Testament alone would be sufficient and in Mohammedan countries, the Koran might be substituted. Masonry does not attempt to interfere with the peculiar religious faith of its disciples, except so far as relates to the belief in the existence of God, and what necessarily results from that belief. The Book of the Law is to the speculative Mason, his spiritual trestle-board, without it, he cannot labor, whatever he believes to be the revealed Will of the Grand Architect constitutes for him this spiritual trestle board and must ever be before him in his hours of speculative labor to be the rule and guide of his conduct. The Landmark therefore requires that a Book of the Law, a religious code of some kind, purporting to be an example of the revealed Will of God, shall form an essential part of the furniture of every Lodge.

COMMENT — Anderson's Book of Constitutions replaced the Charter of the Perestal, when Freemasonry began to spread to other countries. The Holy Bible gradually began to replace the Book of Constitutions. It was found that the book of the sacred law of most countries (at least where Freemasonry was apt to appear) contained the fundamental principles of Masonic Law. The Grand Lodge of England, in 1760, declared the Holy Bible to be a Great Light. Landmark No. 21 is disqualified as a Landmark because the date of the adoption of the Holy Bible is recorded.

Landmark No. 22

THE EQUALITY OF ALL MASONS

...is another Landmark of the Order. This equality has no reference to any subversion to those gradations of rank which might have been instituted by the usages of society. The Monarch, the nobleman, or the gentleman is entitled to all the influence, and receives all the respect which rightly belong to his exalted position. But the doctrine of Masonic equality implies that, as children of one great Father, we meet in the Lodge room on the level —that on the level we are all traveling to one predestined goal, that in the Lodge, genuine merit shall receive more respect than boundless wealth, and that virtue and knowledge alone should be the basis of all Masonic honors and be rewarded with preferment. When the labors of the Lodge are over and the Brethren have retired from their peaceful retreat, to mingle once more with the world, each will then again resume that social position and exercise the privileges of that rank to which the customs of society entitle him.

COMMENT — Masonry regards no man for his material, wealth or station in life. All Masons meet upon the level. Yet it takes nothing for its members, neither honor nor rank. It rather adds to his honor, especially if he has served well among his brethren. All preferment among Masons is grounded upon worth and personal merit.

Mackey, in his political qualifications of a candidate, states that the son of a bondman shall not be admitted as an apprentice and that there never has been any doubt that this was the ancient law and usage of the Order.

Maybe there never has been any doubt where Mackey is concerned but there certainly is doubt in my mind, because it is inconsistent with our teaching concerning social status. He also says the freedman, who was born in slavery, because the servile condition is believed to be (notice his "believed to be") necessarily accompanied by a degradation of mind and an abasement of spirit which unfit them to be recipients of the Sublime doctrines of Freemasonry. This is distinctly the attitude of a snob and is inconsistent with the character of Freemasonry. Our Mother Lodge, the Grand Lodge of England saw the inconsistency of this custom and changed the word freeborn to free. Thus correcting a longstanding disservice to the Order. The point is, we do not take in men whom we consider to be our equal, but we consider all men as being equal.

Landmark No. 23

SECRECY OF THE INSTITUTION

...is another and most important Landmark. There is some difficulty in precisely defining what is meant by a "secret society." If the term refers, as perhaps in strictly logical language it should, to those associations whose designs are concealed from the public eye and whose members are unknown, which produce their results in darkness, and whose operations are carefully hidden from the public gaze, a definition which will be appropriate to many political clubs and revolutionary combinations in despotic countries, where reform, if it is at all to be effected, must be effected by stealth, then clearly Freemasonry is not a secret society. Its design is not publicly proclaimed but is vaunted by its disciples as something to be venerated; its disciples are known. For its membership is considered an honor to be coveted — it works for a result of which it boasts — the civilization and refinement of man, the amelioration of his condition, and the reformation of his manners. But if, by a secret society is meant, and this is the most popular understanding of the term, a society in which there is a certain amount of knowledge, whether it be of methods of recognition or of legendary and traditional learning, which is imparted to those only who have passed through an established form of initiation, the form itself being also concealed or esoteric, then in this sense is Freemasonry undoubtedly a secret society. Now this form of secrecy is a form inherent in it, existing with it from its very foundation, and secured to it by its ancient Landmarks.

If divested of its secret character, it would lose its identity and would cease to be Freemasonry. Whatever objections may therefore be made to the institutions, on account of its secrecy, and however much some unskilled brethren have been willing in times of trial for the sake of expediency, to divest it of its secret character, it will ever be impossible to do so, even were the Landmark not standing before us as an insurmountable obstacle because such change of its character would be social suicide, and the death of the Order would follow its legalized exposure. Freemasonry, as a secret association, has lived unchanged for centuries, as an open society, it would not last for as many years.

COMMENT — We concur with Albert G. Mackey, that the secrecy of the Institution is a Landmark.

Landmark No. 24

THE FOUNDATION OF A SPECULATIVE SCIENCE UPON AN OPERATIVE ART

...and the symbolic use and explanation of the terms of that art, for purposes of religious or moral teaching, constitute another Landmark of the Order. The Temple of Solomon was the cradle of the institution, and therefore, the reference to the operative Masonry, which constructed that magnificent edifice, to the materials and implements which are employed in its construction, and to the artists who were engaged in the building, are all competent and essential parts of the body of Freemasonry, which could not be subtracted from it without an entire destruction of the whole identity of the Order. Hence, all the comparatively modern rules of Masonry, however they may differ in other respects, religiously preserve this Temple history and these operative elements as to the substratum of all their modifications of the Masonic system.

COMMENT — Landmark No. 24 is concurred with.

Landmark No. 25

CAN NEVER BE CHANGED

The last crowning Landmark of all is, that these Landmarks can never be changed. Nothing can be subtracted from them, nothing can be added to them, not the slightest modification can be made in them. As they were received from our predecessors, we are bound by the most solemn obligations of duty to transmit them to our successors. Not one job or title of these unwritten laws can be repealed; for in respect to them, we are not only willing, but compelled to adopt the language of the sturdy old Barons of England —"Nolumus Leges Mutari."

COMMENT — Dr. Mackey says, nothing can be changed, nothing can be subtracted from them and nothing can be added to them. Referring back to Dr. Mackey's discourse on the Landmarks, "They are sufficiently numerous to act as bulwarks against innovation, but not sufficient to stand in the way of needful reform." On one hand he says needful reform can change or alter the Landmarks and on the other hand he says they cannot be changed. Thus Landmark No. 25 is not a Landmark. Those so called Landmarks that have been or can be changed are really not Landmarks at all.

RESPONDENTS

COMMENTS FROM BRO. WALKES

First off, I want to thank Bro. Slaughter for presenting his paper. This is historic as it is the first for Lux e Tenebris Chapter. Unfortunately, I had some problems in reading it due to all of the typographical errors. We should strive to produce papers as free from typing errors as possible, realizing of course that some still will "slip" in, but when we have as many as appeared in Bro. Slaughter's paper, we find ourselves spending as much time trying to figure out exactly what is before us as we do in attempting to answer the same.

This is one of those interesting subjects that has and will continue to be debated by Masonic scholars. Unfortunately, Prince Hall Freemasonry across the board accepted Mackey's Landmarks without giving much thought about Mackey's racism and anti-Prince Hall writings. In 1894, Jno. G. Lewis, Senior, then the C.C.F.C. of Eureka (now Prince Hall) Grand Lodge of Louisiana, who had reluctantly agreed to use Mackey's Jurisprudence as a guide wrote:

> "We are of the opinion that as grand a work or we might say a grander work — one without bias or apparent prejudice, as Mackey's Jurisprudence, could be compiled by some Afro-Mason present in our mind, whose judgments are as valid and reasonings as potent as any in the land. We do not offer this, our view, to detract any worth contained in Mackey's valuable work, not to turn any reader from their perusal and study, but to infer that just as good can be again adduced, and that too, by the Afro-Mason (Black). If a judgment is right, it cannot be more so, no matter who renders it."
>
> (Jno. G. Lewis — End of an Era, Chapter IV, by Walkes)

Prince Hall Freemasonry should know that the "Ahiman Rezon" of the Grand Lodge A.F.M. of South Carolina, compiled by Albert C. Mackey, then Grand Secretary contains:

> "...that a candidate (for the degrees of Freemasonry) must be of free White parents."
>
> (Anti-Negro Legislation in American Masonry by Williamson)

This together with his other anti-Black writings should keep our fraternity from having anything to do with Mackey!

In regards to the paper submitted, I have never accepted Mackey's 25 Landmarks. The Landmarks compiled by him <u>are not fundamental law in Masonry in any sense of the word and should never be accepted or recognized as such for</u>:

A) They were merely the brain child of Mackey.

B) They are unknown outside of North America.

C) They are not recognized nor have they been adopted by all White Grand Lodges in the United States.

D) A number of White Grand Lodges have their own particular series of Landmarks.

1) Book of Constitution of the Grand Lodge of Colorado, edition of 1934, Section 3:

> "By the Ancient Landmarks of Freemasonry, being those unwritten principles of Masonic government and policy which have existed from a time whereof the memory of man runneth not to the contrary and which are among the parts of Masonic law or rules of government which may never be altered or disturbed and by usages and customs which are based upon such landmarks."

2) Book of Constitution of the Grand Lodge of New York, edition of 1932, Section 336:

> This jurisdiction lists six Landmarks.

3) Book of Constitution of the Grand Lodge of Massachusetts, edition of 1950, Section 102:

> This jurisdiction lists seven Landmarks.

4) Caucasian Grand Lodges WITH NO LIST of Landmarks:

> Arizona, Arkansas, Indiana, Iowa, Michigan, Missouri, Nebraska, New Hampshire, North Carolina, Pennsylvania, Rhode Island, Utah, and Washington.

5) Caucasian Grand Lodges WHO ADHERE to the "Old Charges":

> Alabama, Florida, Louisiana, Texas, and Virginia

6) Caucasian Grand Lodges WHO HAVE ADOPTED Mackey's list:

> Delaware, Georgia, Kansas, Maine, Maryland, New Mexico, North Dakota, Oklahoma, Oregon, South Carolina, South Dakota, Wyoming, and District of Columbia.

7) These have "ADOPTED" Mackey "BY CUSTOM" (whatever that means):

> California, Colorado, Idaho, Illinois, Montana, Ohio, Vermont and Wisconsin

8) These Caucasian Grand Lodges have THEIR OWN list of Landmarks:

> Connecticut, Kentucky, Massachusetts, Minnesota, Mississippi, Nevada, New Jersey, New York, Tennessee and West Virginia

> Connecticut has 19 Landmarks as found in the volume "Of Masonic Law and Practice," by Luke A. Lockwood.
>
> Kentucky respects 54 Landmarks
>
> Minnesota has 39
>
> New Jersey has 10
>
> Tennessee has 15
>
> Virginia adheres to the provisions of "Anderson's Constitutions."
>
> West Virginia in 1928, adopted 8

9) Roscoe Pound, former Dean of the Law School at Harvard University in his work bearing the title of "Masonic Jurisprudence," states that the Landmarks of Mackey could be readily reduced to not more than seven in number and cover all of the points involved.

In my opinion, Mackey's No. 6 is fundamentally wrong because to do such does not redound to the prestige of the Fraternity. What truly valid reason can be advanced to sustain such?

In my opinion Mackey's No. 8 is likewise fundamentally wrong and I am well aware of the fact that this is one of a number of "American innovations." This is a Landmark which cannot be used by any Grand Master anywhere outside the Continent of North America. Fundamentally, and from the Masonic point of view, no man can be made a Mason legally nor Masonically except in a just and duly constituted Lodge, he must apply to the same, be investigated and balloted therein.

A man made a Mason at sight is nothing more or less than an "unaffiliated" Mason and no Lodge can be compelled to accept him as a member, not even by the Grand Master.

Mackey's No. 14, is not a "right." Visitation is a privilege and not a right, consequently, it cannot be either demanded or enforced. Visitation is likewise listed as a "courtesy," and one need not admit a visitor to his home except as he so wished, and the visitor cannot go further than to ask the privilege.

Mackey's Nos. 19, 21, and 22, while the Grand Lodge of England requires the Bible on the Altars of its Lodges, it likewise has the Volume of Sacred Law of various other religious beliefs upon the Altars in India, in some parts of that land an Altar will have seven Volumes of Sacred Law reposing thereon.

Damascus Lodge No. 867 (Caucasian) at Brooklyn, New York, has both the Bible and the Koran on its Altar. In view of these facts and without doubt the same custom prevails among the Irish and Scottish Lodges in India. Is there therefore any validity to Nos. 19, 21, and 22 as genuine Masonic Landmarks of Mackey?

By making the Bible a piece of Lodge furniture, the English speaking bodies attempt to "Christianize" the Fraternity and thus remove the alleged "universality" where "men of every country, sect and opinion" can kneel at the same Altar.

Any individual can sit down and compile a set of Landmarks and because they may be put into book form does not give them any Masonic validity. Each Grand Lodge, and especially our Prince Hall Grand Lodges, should determine what sort of Landmarks it shall adhere to.

The only Landmarks that I accept are those listed by Roscoe Pound:

1) Belief in God

2) Belief in the persistence of personality, i.e., the immortality of the soul

3) A "Book of Law" as an indispensable part of the furniture of the Lodge

4) The Legend of the Third Degree

5) Secrecy

6) The symbolism of the operative art

7) That a Mason must be a man, free born and of age!

COMMENTS FROM DONALD C. WHARRY, F.P.S. (Life) Active Member

Dissecting the Landmarks — In this paper there were numerous misspelled words. Documentation of research sources was incomplete in such ways as the author's name was not completed, dates and/or years missing on research sources, quotes not properly documented, and parentheses inappropriately used. Opinions and biases should be limited to Brother Slaughter (he can't interpret opinions about the written work of deceased author — only his opinion). Punctuation vastly incorrect, abbreviation incorrectly done, and in general a below average paper. The suggestions offered to Herman Slaughter are as follows:

1) First, the paper has good potential, but when research is done, it must be clearly and well documented (above average) and grammatically above average.

2) Illustrious Slaughter should send his list of references to someone who will take the list and properly document what has been written by him.

3) Illustrious Slaughter should grammatically redo the complete paper for continuity and format style.

4) When and if all of this is done, this would be a dynamic paper and would be most meritorious to our fraternity.

If I sound curt, I apologize, but if we are to do research as "Lux e Tenebris," then the research must be above average work and/or manuscripts, without a doubt, due to negative comments coming out of the Ohio Jurisdiction.

Williamson's "Out of the Past"

by Joseph A. Walkes, Jr., FPS
(1st Edition, 1983-84)

While reviewing some of the material that I have on Bro. Harry A. Williamson, the great Prince Hall Masonic scholar, I ran across an article by him "Out of the Past," in which he presented very brief quotes from various items presented from an early Caucasian publication called The Freemason's Monthly Magazine. Brother Williamson had come into possession of a total of 32 volumes, beginning with issue No. 2, Volume 1, dated December 1, 1841 with the last being, Volume 32, for the year 1873.

The publication was edited by Charles W. Montpelier, who was the Grand Secretary of the Caucasian Grand Lodge of Massachusetts from 1834 to 1867.

Following his death in 1873, the Rev. Charles H. Titus, his successor as Grand Secretary, together with Sereno D. Nickerson, who was Grand Master from 1872 to 1874, began the publication of the successor to Moore's publication, it being renamed The New England Freemason. Brother Williamson discovered a great deal of material of interest to Prince Hall Freemasonry, but only presented very short descriptions, without comments, which did not allow the readers to digest the full scope of material.

I have decided to amplify the material by presenting as much of the text taken from the two publications as I can. I also plan to leave as much of Williamson's descriptions as possible, while adding some of my views on the subject.

VOLUME V (December 1, 1845, pg. 46)

(Williamson's Text) This is a lengthy letter to the editor of The Freemason's Quarterly Review and in short is the story about a Captain D whose ship lying at Camma, West Africa, had an altercation with some Spanish slave traders and native tribesmen. Captain D discovered one of the Spaniards had a neck-handkerchief upon which was a Masonic emblem and he gave a Masonic sign which was promptly answered with the result this Spaniard brought his employees to the defense of Captain D.

(From the Publication) "It is unnecessary to remind Freemasons that our private signals, although of great importance, are not the most valuable, nor the most interesting parts of the science we endeavor to cultivate. Masonry embraces a wider range, and has a nobler object in view; namely, the cultivation and improvement of the understanding, and affections. But that the methods by which Masons recognize each other have, frequently, the most important consequences, will be illustrated...and which...will show that Freemasonry exerts the highest influence of even the most uncultivated and ignorant who adopt its principles.

In the case I am about to relate, we find a man, whose trade it was to kidnap his fellow creatures, flesh and blood like himself, for the purpose of selling them, and dooming them to the most miserable destiny for life, if they were so unfortunate as to survive the voyage across the wide ocean, in a slave-ship, whose very occupation must have made him brutal, if not ferocious, we find him, I say, practically acknowledging the force of his obligations as a Freemason, and rendering due homage to the great moral lessons he had learnt in that character."

(Walkes' Comments) This has to be an indictment of Caucasian Freemasonry, for to make a slave-trader a Freemason, is an insult to the concept of Freemasonry, and yet there were many slave-owners who took the obligation upon the altar of Freemasonry, such as George Washington.

VOLUME V (February 1, 1846, pg. 112)

(Williamson's Text) Under the title of "The Black Mason" there is the translation from the French of the story of a black man in one of the French colonies who performed great service upon the occasion of an earthquake. The man, Aime Confiance, was a slave but as a reward for his heroism, the governor of the colony obtained his freedom and he was sent to France where in due course he was made a Freemason. Five pages are devoted to the story but at no time has either the name of the governor, of the colony, nor its location been mentioned.

(From the Publication) "In one of those too frequent calamities whereof our colonies are victims, a black performed prodigies of courage. Gifted with an extraordinary energy and supernatural strength, he snatched from the flames, or drew from the rubbish heaped up by the earthquake, more than twenty persons, whom the bravest regarded as lost, and dreamed not of saving, so difficult did the task appear to them, and so desperate might have been the attempt. But the black calculated not; he boldly rushed wherever a recent damage, a cry, or the least indication led to the supposition that a human being could yet breathe. He performed, as I before said, miracles; but the greatest of all, was that which God performed in preserving him, unharmed, from so many dangers, blindly braved. Heaven saved the life of him who had saved so many lives.

The crisis passed, Aime Confiance — so the black was called — went to resume his painful task. But his generous conduct had been remarked, and everybody conceived that the yoke of servitude could not bear down his noble head. The governor, by authority, negotiated for his redemption; and to complete the good office, the Lodge X ---, was pleased to bestow on him the means of quitting the colonies, where the prejudice against color created a delicate and difficult position for a freed slave. Accordingly, the respectable Lodge voted a sum sufficient to carry him to France, where one of the five Lodges secured for him an agricultural employment.

The Lodge, as the highest testimony of the public gratitude and its particular sympathy, was pleased to initiate him before his departure — a great and unusual favor, of which Confiance must since have understood the value. Thus Masonry put in practice, at the same time, two of its fundamental principles — equality and beneficence: equality, in making, in that land of bondage, a Brother of one recently a slave; beneficence, in honoring courageous devotion.

On the day fixed for his initiation, Confiance was conducted into the cabinet of reflection, by a skillful Brother, one of the most honorable inhabitants of the colony. "Confiance," said this Brother to him, before again shutting the mysterious gate upon him, "study to render thyself worthy of the liberty which you already hath possess, and into which you are now going in reality to enter."

Some days after, Confiance set sail for France. After his departure it was understood that the money which had been given him by the Lodge, had been employed by him in purchasing another slave, his companion in suffering, a poor old man whom his master was willing to sell for a small consideration. Confiance was received gratuitously on board the vessel, on his consenting to work his passage.

Three years have elapsed since his arrival, and he no longer distrusts French liberty. All the peasants and workmen by whom he is surrounded, love and respect him. It only remains for us to say, that he has already saved the lives of three rash persons, who were nearly drowned while bathing in the river on whose bank his cottage is situated. He has received a royal medal from the hands of the Prefect; and is more over desired that he should be admitted into the Lodge of the town. He is known among the initiated as the Black Mason.

(Walkes' Comments) The narrator also tells the interesting story of one Benedict, a Black who had journeyed through France. It is also a most interesting story. Confiance was initiated by the governor of the colony, and the first to hold out his hand to him was the son of his "master."

(Williamson's Text) Under the title of "African Lodge, In Boston," there is the copy of a letter from the Grand Secretary of New York to Montpelier of Massachusetts concerning Boyer Lodge No. 1, in New York City, also about African Grand Lodge of Massachusetts. The latter Grand Secretary replied under date of July 26, 1845, that he had interviewed John T. Hilton, Master of African Lodge No. 459, who informed him there was some controversy between it and Boyer Lodge and they would have nothing to do with the latter.

(From the Publication) "Our readers will recollect that about a year ago we had occasion, in reply to inquiries at that time addressed to us, to refer to the existence of the African Lodge in this city. Among the letters then received, asking for information on the subject, was one from the late Grand Secretary of the Grand Lodge of New York — our answer to which will be found incorporated in the following report, adopted by that Grand Body, at its annual session in June last:

> To The M.W. Grand Lodge of the State of New York:
>
> The undersigned, to whom was committed the memorial of a number of persons forming a Lodge in this city, called Boyer Lodge No. 1, presented to this Grand Lodge in June last, has to report that, according to instructions, has inquired into the facts set forth in said memorial, and finds that the memorialists have been entirely ignorant of Masonic history, and of their own particular history or otherwise that they very deliberately attempted to impose upon this Grand Lodge as historical facts, what they knew to be untrue.
>
> Said memorial sets forth, 'that the Boyer Lodge No. 1 of the City of New York had been some nineteen or twenty years regularly and legally constituted and installed, as a Master Mason Lodge, with a legal Warrant or Charter, issued by the Rt. W. African Grand Lodge of Ancient Free and Accepted Masons of the City of Boston, in the State of Massachusetts, whose Charter empowering them to Charter Lodges in the United States of America, is from the M.W. Grand Lodge of Free and Accepted Masons of Scotland, and is now half a century old, and dated the 29th September, A.D. 1784, and of Masonry, 5784, Robert Rolf G.M. and William White, Grand Secretary, with the seal of the M.W.G. Lodge of Free and Accepted Masons of London, signed by Lord Howard, Earl of Effingham, then acting as Grand Master, under his Royal Highness, Henry Frederick of Cumberland.' This single sentence presents a mass of gross absurdities of false facts; mingling in the Fraternity of the African Lodge in Boston, the Grand Lodges then in England, and the Grand Lodge in Scotland.

To correct this statement, in part, the memorialists have recently presented their paper, in which they say: 'We beg leave to state, that the Boyer Lodge, petitioning your honorable Body in May last, that they fell into an error, if they said that the African Grand Lodge of Boston, who Chartered us, received their Charter from the Grand Lodge of Scotland, we only intended to state that we were _____that they petitioned that body for a Charter, and in due time received a hearing from the Grand Seal of London, &c. &c. We have recently received a letter from our Correspondent and Brother, Robert T. Crucefix, stating that the Charter, granted to the African Grand Lodge of Boston, by the Grand Lodge of England, in the year 1784, and was numbered 459, and that the Grand Lodge of Scotland had 'nothing to do with it.' They then insert an extract of a letter from Dr. Crucefix, in which it will be noticed he does not call it 'The African Grand Lodge' as above set forth, but says that 'The African Lodge of Boston' received its warrant from the Grand Lodge of England, in the year 1784, and was numbered 459, on the Registry. The Warrant was signed by Rowland Holt, D.G. Master and countersigned by William White, Grand Secretary, the father of our present Secretary. This I find all regularly entered in the books of our Grand Lodge; consequently, any connection with the Grand Lodge of Scotland is out of the question.

The undersigned having requested the Rt. W. Charles W. Montpelier, Grand Secretary of the Grand Lodge of Massachusetts, to endeavor to see the Charter of the so-called African Grand Lodge of Boston, and if possible, obtain a copy thereof, begs leave to incorporate the following extract from Brother Moore's letter, dated July 26, 1845:

> I called, agreeably to your request, on Mr. Hilton, who, I believe, is the Master of the African Lodge in this city, — stated to him the object of my visit, and asked permission to see the Charter of his Lodge. He informed me that there was a difficulty between his and Boyer Lodge, of long standing, — that they had nothing to do with that Lodge, nor would they have, until the difference referred to was settled. He further stated, that they were entirely independent of all <u>white</u> Lodges, asked no favors of them, <u>and would have nothing to do with them</u>; nor would they admit a white Mason, if he should present himself as a visitor. In the course of the conversation, he distinctly said, that he had been '<u>told by them people</u>,' (meaning Boyer Lodge), to have no communication with anybody on the subject of their recognition by the Grand Lodge of New York. He <u>also and positively and repeatedly refused to allow me to see the Charter of his Lodge, or to give me any information in relation to its history or present existence</u>. It is proper for me to add, that my conversation with him was kind and gentle. I explicitly stated to him that I did not call <u>officially</u>, but as a friend, and at your request, with a view to ascertain whether Boyer Lodge was a regularly constituted Lodge, such as the Grand Lodge of New York would recognize.

This Lodge (African), has unquestionably, a Charter of some kind. Twenty years ago I saw it; and my impression is, that it is an ordinary Lodge Charter; but whether genuine or not, I am unable to say. I have understood that it was surreptitiously obtained, (through the agency of a Sea Captain), from one of the two Grand Lodges then in England; but I can find no such record in the proceedings of either of those bodies. I have a list of the Lodges chartered by the Grand Lodge of Scotland, up to 1804. It contains the name of St. Andrew's Lodge, in Boston chartered in 1756, but it does not bear the name of African Lodge, nor does it furnish any evidence, nor have I ever met with any, (to my recollection), that the Grand Lodge of Scotland ever granted a Charter for more than one Lodge in Boston, Vis: St. Andrews. The only Provincial Grand Lodge ever formed in Massachusetts, under authority derived from the Grand Lodge of Scotland, was that over which General Warren presided, in 1769 — and the only one by authority from England was St. John's Grand Lodge, in 1733. If there be others, claiming such powers, they are spurious.

The African Lodge has never been recognized by the Grand Lodge of this Commonwealth. Applications have several times been made by its members for admission to our Lodges, but they have generally, if not always, been refused. Mr. Hilton stated to me, that he had once, through the influence of a friend, gained admission into one of our out-of-town Lodges. If so, the Brother who introduced him, laid himself upon to censure, and would have been dealt with, had the circumstance come to the knowledge of the Grand Lodge. That the course of our Grand Lodge, in reference to African Lodge, is not the result of prejudice, it is only necessary for me to say, that within the last month, a colored Brother from England, has visited, and been kindly received, in one of our city Lodges. Such is the state of the case, so far as I am able to communicate it. The argument does not belong to me; but you will permit me to inquire, whether your Grand Lodge is prepared to recognize any real or pretended Lodge, existing within another jurisdiction, before it has been recognized by the Grand Lodge of that jurisdiction? Again, does your Grand Lodge allow other Grand Lodges to establish Lodges within its jurisdiction? And is it ready to recognize Lodges so established?

These three questions have been, by repeated decision of this Grand Lodge, answered in the negative; and according to the treaty stipulations entered into by this, and other Grand Lodges of this continent, soon after the revolution, and the uniform resistance of every encroachment upon the sole jurisdiction of the several Grand Lodges, down to the present time; these questions can be answered only in the negative.

The undersigned would further state, that the legality of the Body called Boyer Lodge No. 1, has been already twice reported on by Committees of this Grand Lodge; on the 3rd of March 1812, and on the 4th of March 1829; in the latter report the main facts were correctly stated, and able argument sustained, and the conclusion drawn, that Boyer Lodge No. 1, can be regarded only as a clandestine Lodge; the undersigned can arrive only at the same conclusion, it being established beyond doubt, that the African Lodge at Boston, was illegally established by the Grand Lodge of England, within the jurisdiction of the Grand Lodge of England, that its assumed authority to grant Warrants was unmasonic and fraudulent; and further that the statement contained in the memorial of said Boyer Lodge, that it has been 'regularly and legally constituted and installed as a Master Mason's Lodge, with a legal Warrant or Charter,' is totally unfounded.

All of which is respectfully submitted.

JAMES HERRING, Grand Secretary

New York, June 2, 1846

Since writing the letter from which the extract in the foregoing, a friend and Brother has handed us the following document, which was published in the papers of this city in 1827, but had entirely escaped our recollection. We give it as an important part of history of the Lodge in question:

(What follows is the celebrated declaration of Independence issued June 18, 1827 bearing the signatures of the Masters, Wardens and Secretary of African Lodge No. 459).

(Walkes' Comments) Harry E. Davis writes in his History, that Boyer Lodge, the first Black Lodge, was established in New York City in 1812 under a charter from Prince Hall Grand Lodge, and the same year it appears that some overtures were made to the (Caucasian) Grand Lodge of New York for recognition. Davis records the incidents noted above on pages 135 to 137. John T. Hilton as far as I am concerned took the right course in denying the Caucasians a look at the Warrant of African Lodge 459, for attempts may have been made at the early time to destroy the charter. Hilton's statement that the Lodge was independent of whites is of importance. While Caucasians refuse to understand that there are two Americas, one white, the other Black; and the Jurisdiction of the Caucasian Grand Lodge of Massachusetts did not extend into Black America brings the entire issue into better understanding.

VOLUME VII (July 1, 1848, pg. 262)

(From the Publication)

African Grand Lodge

We understand that a body of colored persons has recently been organized in this city, under the name of 'Prince Hall Grand Lodge.' It claims to be a Masonic body, and to have under its jurisdiction one or more subordinate Lodges, and, we believe, one or more Chapters; or at all events, there are colored persons connected with it, who claim to be R.A. Masons. We understand, also, that they derive their authority to form a Grand Lodge from a body, located either in New York or Philadelphia, styling itself the 'General Grand Lodge of the United States.' This is about all we know respecting the matter; and our object in referring to it at this time, is merely to say, that there are no Lodges of colored Masons in this city, or any other part of the United States, that are recognized and acknowledged by the Grand Lodge of Massachusetts, or, to our knowledge, by any other regularly constituted Grand Lodge in this country; and the same thing is true, so far as we are informed, as regards to chapters, and all other Masonic bodies. We have thought the statement of this fact important, in order that our Brethren in distant States may not be imposed upon.

We sometime since gave the history of the establishment of the 'African Lodge' of colored persons in this city. The facts were then fully and correctly stated, and need not now therefore, be repeated. The Charter was granted in 1784, though not received until 1787. It was obtained by a Captain Scott, master of a London packet, sailing out of this port. We have always understood that Scott represented to the authorities at London, (the Duke of Cumberland being Grand Master), that the petitioners at London, (the Duke of Cumberland being Grand Master), were white persons, and that on the strength of his misrepresentations in this and other respects, the Charter, after having been withheld for two or three years subsequent to its date, was finally sent out, and the Lodge was organized under the immediate auspices of Mr. Prince Hall, a colored person, at that time of some distinction among his own people in his city. It was never recognized by the Grand Lodge of this State; nor has there ever been any Masonic intercourse between the two bodies.

(Williamson's Comments) "...how could there have been any misrepresentation as to the identity of the petitioners because of the name 'African,' surely, there were not any white Africans in Boston at that time."

(Walkes' Comments) As we can see our Caucasian writers do not mind stretching the truth. It is generally known that Prince Hall addressed a letter to William Moody, Master of Brotherly Love Lodge No. 55, London:

> Dear Brother, I would inform you that this Lodge hath been founded almost eight years and we have had only a permit to Walk on St John's Day and to Bury our Dead in Manner and Form before now, though we have been importuned to send to France for one, yet we thought it best to send to the Fountain from whence we received the Light for a Warrant: and now Dear Brother we must take you our advocate at the Grand Lodge; who we hope will not deny us nor treat us Beneath the rest of our fellowmen, although Poor yet Sincere Brethren of the Craft, etc.

The Grand Lodge of England book covering the period September 1790 to January 1818 is missing, and no doubt, if it could be found, it could clear up many of the issues that none of us are sure of. Yet our Caucasian counterparts will use any bit of misinformation to discredit Prince Hall Freemasonry, as can be seen by the above.

VOLUME XII (June 1, 1853, page 233)

(Williamson's Text) The title of this contribution is "Negro Lodges" and proposes to give an account of the same and the editor "believes" a Lodge of Negroes is operating in Boston and in other sections of the country.

(From the Publication)

NEGRO LODGES

The Committee on Foreign Correspondence in the Grand Lodge of Mississippi, takes an extract from the address of the Grand Master of the Grand Lodge of Texas, and comments upon it as though the country was full of regularly authorized negro Lodges. The Committee says, either the Grand Lodges of England and Ireland 'have invaded the jurisdiction of some of our sister Grand Lodges in the United States, with or without consent of these Grand Lodges, or our sisters have themselves been guilty of wrong.' Neither of these alternatives is true, and the filing at 'our sisters' was uncalled for. There is not a lawfully authorized or acknowledged negro Lodge in the United States, nor are we aware that there is a negro in the country, who could rightfully claim, or properly be admitted into any lawful Masonic Lodge. They exist in this city, and in New York, in Philadelphia and in Baltimore, and probably in other cities, south and west; but they exist without authority, and their claims are nowhere recognized.

The assumption of the name does not make them Masonic; and it is an assumption for which there is no remedy. Why then keep agitating the subject? No good can come out of it. It is one with which our Grand Lodges have nothing to do. The evil does not exist, in a form approachable by them, or over which they can extend their authority. We have so often given the history of the only black Lodge ever organized in this country, under anything which could be construed into lawful authority, that we had supposed it was familiar to every intelligent Brother. But in this it seems we were mistaken. It may not, therefore be wholly unprofitable to repeat, that in the year 1784, a petition was sent out to the Grand Lodge at London, by some colored persons in this city, praying for a Charter authorizing them to open a Masonic Lodge. The petition was entrusted to a Captain Scott, master of a London packet, sailing out of this port, through whose influence and as alleged, misrepresentations, the prayer of the petitioners was granted. The Charter was not, however, received until 1787, when we believe, the Lodge was organized, though we are not aware that it ever did any work. Its existence was of short duration; and as it had been illegally authorized by the Grand Lodge of England, it was soon after stricken from the register of that body. Such was the beginning and the end of the only Lodge of colored Masons ever opened in America, under the sanction of any acknowledged Grand Lodge in the world. It was never recognized by the Grand Lodge of this Commonwealth, nor was any intercourse ever allowed with its members.

Some years since, this old Charter fell into the hands of certain colored persons claiming to be Masons, by whom a Lodge was organized in this city. We believe it is still in existence, though of its character and the nature of its proceedings we know nothing. If its members are in the possession of anything resembling the ritual of Masonry, they probably received it from the West Indies or St. Domingo, where the more intelligent and educated of their race are not refused admission into the Lodges. President Boyer was a Mason, as were also most of the members of his government. It is likewise probable that from this quarter has nearly all the black Masonry in this country been derived. But from whatever source it may have emanated, it is all spurious, and in no manner identified with the legitimate Freemasonry in the United States; nor is any Grand Lodge in the Union accountable for its existence or continuance. The insinuation that the Grand Lodge of a sister State would, under any circumstances, countenance a gross violation of the conceded rule in relation to this class of persons, is ungenerous.

But enough. The subject is not a suitable one for discussion in our pages, nor in the reports of committees of correspondence; at least not until it shall assume some more tangible shape than it at present bears.

(Walkes' Comments) Back in 1973, I had asked John M. Sherman of the Caucasian Grand Lodge of Massachusetts to check the Massachusetts Register to see if the African Lodge was publishing information as to its meetings. On the 10th of November of that year, he answered:

> Referring to the data in the Massachusetts Register of 1806, I found we had what appears to be a complete set of the annual issues from 1802 to around 1840, so I looked at the issues for each year, 1802-1817, to see what they showed regarding

African Lodge and found the following: It was mentioned in every year from 1702 (sic 1802) — 1813, and dropped after that. The notice would read 'African Lodge in Boston meets regularly at (see below)...on the evening of the last Tuesday of each month." The places given where it met were as follows: 1802, 1803 — at the sign of the Golden Fleece; 1804, 1805 — in Kilby Street; 1806 — at the house of Prince Hall on Congress Street; and 1807 — 1813, inclusive - place not given.

I have selected pages reproduced from The Massachusetts Register and United States Calender, 1806, published by John West and Manning & Son, sold wholesale and retail at their bookstores, Conhill, Boston, which shows on page 47 under Masonic Societies, the Grand Lodge of Massachusetts (Caucasian) which names all of the Grand Lodge officers, and from page 48 through page 51 names all of the Districts and the Lodges therein, as well as the Grand Royal Arch Chapter. This is followed on page 51 by "The African Lodge" in Boston meets regularly at the house of Prince Hall, in Congress Street, on the evening of the first Tuesday in each month." Yet the writer of the article writes "...we are not aware that it ever did any work." Also, the proceedings of the Caucasian Grand Lodge of Massachusetts, Quarterly Communication, September 13, 1876, carries the so called "Woodbury Report" named after Charles Levi Woodbury, which concerns the Prince Hall Grand Lodge of Ohio and the Caucasian Grand Lodge of Ohio. There is also carried an Appendix taken from the Freemason's Magazine, Boston, March 1847; the same publication we are presently reviewing. The Proceedings further carries, "Report made to the Grand Lodge of Massachusetts," December 8, 1869, on the Petition of Lewis Hayden and others. Lewis Hayden, of course, was the Grand Master of the Prince Hall Grand Lodge of Massachusetts. It would seem while the author of the article "believed" that there was a Lodge of Blacks in Boston, his Grand Lodge, and everybody else, knew it.

VOLUME XII (July 1, 1853, page 295)

(Williamson Text) In an article bearing the same caption as above, some Mason in Mississippi took exception to remarks by the editor concerning matters on the subject expressed by the Fraternal Correspondent of the Southern body.

In the same contribution one is surprised to read that in 1852, the President of the Republic of Liberia forwarded a petition to the Grand Lodge of the District of Columbia (Caucasian) for a Charter for a Lodge in the former country but the American Grand body took no action in the matter.

There is further discussion by the editor relative to the exception taken by his Mississippi Brother and one learns that in 1846, the Grand Lodge of Illinois penalized the Master of a Lodge in Chicago, which had admitted a Freemason as a visitor whose mother was a Cherokee Indian but whose father was a mulatto.

(From the Publication)

NEGRO LODGES

We give place to the following communication, in compliance with the wishes of the estimable Brother whose name is appended to it. Had he placed discretionary power in our hands, our conviction of the great danger of agitating such a subject would have induced us to withhold its publication. But having no such discretion, we lay it before our readers, permissing, that we shall not again betrude the matter upon their notice. However, our correspondent may regard that the subject is neither a safe nor a profitable one for discussion in our pages, nor in the proceedings of Grand Lodges. Whether our opinion in this respect is right or wrong, is immaterial. It is based on our judgment, and must be allowed to influence our action. We give his communication, with a few and brief notes as are consistent with the position in which we most unexpectedly find ourselves:

Natchez, June 14, 1853

Dear Brother Montpelier:

Your June number of Magazine is before me. Your comments on the part of the report of Committee on Foreign Correspondence in Mississippi, relating to negro Lodges, has been read with some surprise. I allude to the tone of the article, more particularly:

1) A simple statement of facts derived from other sources and what was considered a legitimate conclusion therefrom, is construed by you into 'a fling,' and that 'uncalled for,' at our sister Grand Lodges. To fling means, literally, "to throw," and if the Committee hit any other Grand Lodge than their own, it must certainly be a 'fling'; but modern use has attached the idea to "little malice or ill will." I trust the Mississippi Committee has too much regard for their individual character and for the dignity of their office, as well as a too high respect for other Grand Lodges in the United States, to say anything in a malevolent spirit, or under other inspiration than that of the highest motive;

2) Whether their comments were uncalled for, is a matter of opinion, and though I do not think that that difference of opinion, which might be expect-

ed to exist on this subject, has been expressed by you in the kindest and most charitable manner, I am willing, for one, to allow you considerable latitude on this subject;

3) But why the Mississippi Committee should voluntarily do an uncalled for act, which act could only inflict pain on themselves, and in which no sinister motive could be traced, must be referred to other philosophy than mine to determine. If you had published the whole of the Committee's remarks on the subject of negroes and negro Lodges, and they would have occupied but little of your space, I would not have had occasion to write this letter;

4) Certainly not to defend the Committee for introducing the subject of negro Masons and negro Lodges into their report; for the Committee showed that the subject was before the Grand Lodges of the District of Columbia, Illinois, Texas and New Hampshire, in 1852. The Grand Lodge of Texas passed a special resolution on the subject, as also did the Grand Lodge of Illinois, and it's the Grand Lodge of Mississippi alone to keep silence and not comment upon these proceedings, nor upon the improper position of the Grand Lodge of New Hampshire? And why the Grand Lodge of Mississippi and not the Grand Lodge of Texas and Illinois, which preceded the former in agitating the matter, was the subject of your comments, it might satisfy curiosity, though utility might not be the gainer, to inquire. I will let that pass.

5) Now a word upon the facts of the case. The committee in considering the proceedings of the Grand Lodges above mentioned, said 'either the Grand Lodge of England or Ireland have invaded the jurisdiction of some of our sister Grand Lodges in the United States, with or without the consent of these Grand Lodges, or our sisters have themselves been guilty or wrong.' On what was this opinion founded? By referring to their report, it will be seen that in 1845-1846, negroes had visited Lodges in Illinois — and again in that State, last year; and this last visitor, it appears, presented certificates of his having visited Lodges in Kentucky, Missouri, Wisconsin and Ohio, and he also showed a constitution and By-Laws of his Lodge, representing them as deriving authority from the "North American Grand Lodge."

6) It may be said, and said truly, that the North American Grand Lodge is not a legally constituted body, and you say, 'there is not a lawfully authorized or acknowledged negro Lodge in the United States, nor are we aware that there is a negro in the country, who could rightfully claim or be admitted into any lawful Masonic Lodge.' That is precisely the opinion of the Committee of Mississippi, very fully and handsomely expressed, and I would only add,

whether the Lodges were chartered, or the individuals initiated, by Grand Lodges in Great Britain or America. You say, that 'there are associations of blacks claiming to be Masonic, is true; but they exist without authority and their claims are nowhere recognized.' You will certainly not consider me impertinent, for inquiring by what means the blacks above mentioned visited the Lodges in Illinois in 1845-1846, when the only question raised, in the discussion which resulted from their visitation, was that of expediency, and not one word was said about their want of legal qualification. If he who visited the Lodges in Illinois, Kentucky, Missouri, Wisconsin and Ohio last year, did so only on the strength of the constitution and By-Laws of a Lodge deriving their authority from 'the North American Grand Lodge,' did so illegally, and certainly the remarks of the committee in this respect were not uncalled for, nor the subject 'unsuited to the reports of the Committees on Foreign Correspondence.' But in 1845-1846, the legality of the Lodge and the regularity of the initiation were not questioned. In addition to this, the Grand Master of Texas, whose words were quoted by the committee, and which paper I believe you reviewed last year, without contradiction, I plead as a full justification of the committee of Mississippi.

It will doubtless astonish many of the Brethern to learn that there are now, in several of the eastern and north-western States, bodies of negroes, who profess to be working, as regular Lodges, under Charters from the Grand Lodge of England and from other sources.

Again, he says; 'through the report of the Committee on Foreign Correspondence of the Grand Lodge of New York, we learn that there are one or more such Lodges in New York City, one in Cincinnati, one in St. Louis, one or more in New Jersey, one in Chillicothe, Ohio and others in Philadelphia.'

Were the remarks of the Committee uncalled for? That the subject is 'unworthy of the report, ' is no fault of the Committee, but of those who furnished it. But why? Let those answer who are the cause.

Fraternally yours,

WILLIAM P. MELLEN,
One of the Committee of Mississippi

1) The article which our Brother is pleased to consider an attack upon his report, is a frank and plain statement of the origin and existence among us, of what are called negro Lodges, and of the light in which they, and negro Masons are regarded by the Grand Lodges in this country. Though elicited by the report submitted to the Grand Lodge of Mississippi, it is general in its terms and application, with the slightest exceptions hereafter noticed. Entertaining the belief that there existed a great misapprehension of the true character of the bodies in question, and of the relation they hold to the Masonic family, the light in which they are regarded by our Brethren who's misfortune it is to have them in their midst, and foreseeing that any serious misunderstanding on a subject so delicate, must inevitably end in consequences highly prejudicial to the peace of the Fraternity, we deemed it our duty, as public journalists, not only to show that there were no present grounds for uneasiness, but to tenter a protest against the agitation of the subject, and 'uncalled for,' until it shall assume a more tangible shape than it at present bears. To the propriety of this course, we think no right minded and true Mason can or would desire to take exception. Our Brother has misconceived our purpose, or he has incautiously surrendered his generally good judgment to his acute sensitiveness on the subject. In this last respect, we are willing to allow him 'considerable latitude.'

2) We object to so much of this small criticism, as would make us impute even a 'little malice' or 'a malevolent spirit,' to the committee. Our Brother intended to do just what his words have done, 'hit' those of 'our sisters' (i.e. Grand Lodges), who, as he alleges, in the event that the Grand Lodges of England and Ireland have not invaded their jurisdictions in establishing negro Lodges, 'have themselves been guilty of wrong.' We are charitable enough to believe that our Brother intended no more by his 'hit' than did Dean Swift by his 'fling' when he wrote:

I, who love to have a fling,
Both at senate house and king.

3) This difference of opinion may be stated thus: If any of our Brethren think it a part of the duty of committees on correspondence to scatter firebrands throughout the length and breadth of the Masonic community, we, on the contrary, think such incendiary work, 'uncalled for.' That is the difference, in a nut-shell — its latitude and longitude.

4) The reason we did not publish this part of the report, is that we thought it based on a misapprehension of the facts; and that consequently, its conclusions were not just. We conceived that we were doing all that was necessary or expedient to do in

the matter, in making a simple reference to the report, and giving the facts as they really exist. There is no difference of opinion between us and our Brother on the main questions; and should the time ever come when it shall be necessary to meet it, he will find us by his side. We cannot, however, consent to play the part of the hero of Cervantes.

5) The subject was brought before the Grand Lodge of the District of Columbia in 1852, on a petition from the President of Liberia, for a Charter for a Lodge in that Republic. The Grand Lodge took no official action upon it — 'the subject matter having been already disposed of.' Was this a cause of uneasiness? Let us look at the subject in all its bearings — look at Liberia as it is — see who its friends are and where they are found, and we shall have little difficulty in coming to the conclusion, that the cause is not one which calls for an inadversion. Neither does it furnish any grounds for the apprehension that other similar bodies are about to pursue an opposite course. This case therefore does not help our Brother's argument. On the contrary, it makes against it, inasmuch as it proves, that in this, as in the only other instance in this country, so far as we are informed, where a petition has ever been presented for a charter for a Lodge of colored Masons, it was promptly rejected. We are not aware that the subject was before the Grand Lodge of Illinois in 1852. That body in 1846, disposed of the question in a manner which ought to be satisfactory to our declaring, 'that this Grand Lodge is unqualifiedly opposed to the admission of negroes or mulattoes into Lodges under this jurisdiction.' The violation of this rule is also made to operate a forfeiture of the Charter.

The subject was brought before the Grand Lodge of Texas the last year, by the Grand Master, in his address quoted as follows:

> It will doubtless astonish many of the Brethren to learn that there are now, in several of the Eastern and Northwestern States, bodies of negroes, who profess to be working as regular Lodges under Charters from the Grand Lodge of England and from other sources.
>
> The propriety of the action of the bodies, who have so far desecrated our time-honored institution as to issue these Charters, is not a subject to be discussed. This, as well as every other Grand Lodge within the slave holding States, should indignantly protest against all procedure of the sort, and demand the immediate annulment of all Charters which have been granted.

Had the Grand Master of Texas been correctly informed as to the facts in the case, he would not probably have expressed himself in precisely these terms. In the first place, the Grand Lodge of England has granted no charters for Lodges in America, during the present century. This part of the 'profession' was therefore false, and wholly unworthy of his official notice, besides its injustice to the Grand Lodge of England. In the second place, there is not a negro Lodge in the country, working under a charter, having the sanction of any regular Grand Lodge in the world.

If such Lodges have any charters at all, they are derived from self-constituted spurious negro associations, calling themselves Grand Lodges; over which the regular Masonic authorities of this country, have no more control or power, than they have over the secret "Triad Brotherhood" of China; and of the true character of which they know so little. What then, would our 'indignant protest' amount to? And whom shall we demand 'their immediate annulment'? Is not this running a tilt against a windmill? And yet our Brother of Mississippi takes up the strain, and charges the Grand Lodge of England with having commenced the evil 'in the spirit of abolition fanaticism' by striking out the words 'free born' from the ritual. The Grand Lodge of England undoubtedly, in this last respect, 'removed one of the ancient and valued Landmarks of Freemasonry'; but we are at a loss to understand how that act, which took place but two or three years ago, was the commencement of the evil of negro Masonry in this country; for it has existed in our midst half a century. He says, in continuation, that 'Ireland followed in her footsteps,' a fact of which we were not aware, and adds that 'either these Grand Lodges have invaded the jurisdiction of our sister Grand Lodges in the United States, with or without the consent of these Grand Lodges, or our sisters have themselves been guilty of wrong.' We will 'let that pass,' but we must still adhere to our first opinion, that the 'fling' was 'uncalled for.'

One word touching the Grand Lodge of New Hampshire. The committee of correspondence in 1852, opened a new question, and justly exposed themselves to criticism. Their own Grand Lodge however took no action on the subject. It was a question about which there is, and probably will continue to be, a difference of opinion. But the case supposed is one not likely to arise, and its agitation was therefore premature and ill-advised. Our Brother of Mississippi may rightfully plead justification, of his 'off-set' here.

6) Our Brother has run fairly off the track here. The report charges that 'our sister' Grand Lodges 'have been guilty of wrong.' He now abandons this ground as untenable, and transfers his accusation to certain subordinate Lodges. On this point we have no controversy. But how stands the case in the new aspect in which he presents it? In 1845-1846, a mulatto (we think it was a single case), born of a Cherokee mother, and therefore 'free born' and in point of law an Indian, though his father was an African, was admitted once as a visitor, into a Lodge of Chicago.

What was the consequence? The Lodges in the State rose almost en masse against it, and their Grand Master, who was supposed to have favored the admission, and though he was subsequently exonerated of any immediate agency in the matter, cost him his influence among his Brethren. The Grand Lodge took the case in hand; and so far from treating it as a question of 'expediency,' as said by our correspondent, passed the stringent resolutions referred to in the preceding note. The language of the committee who reported the resolutions was this — '*The Author of All* has placed a distinguishing mark upon them (negroes), clearly indicating that there was a distinctiveness to be kept up; and it is repulsive to the finest feelings of the heart, to think that between them and us there can be a mutual reciprocity of all social privileges.' Does our Brother hold that this Grand Lodge, in the course it pursued on that occasion, was 'guilty of wrong'? 'It might satisfy curiosity, though utility might not be the gainer,' to inquire why this long buried case was exhumed? It certainly does not help our Brother's argument, for the Grand Lodge of Illinois stood up squarely on his own ground. So much for the first cause of grievance in his catalogue of 'facts.'

His next complaint is that a negro was, the last year, admitted into the Lodge in Illinois. We have not the proceedings of the Grand Lodge of that State for October 1852, before us, and are a little surprised that our Brother should have had them when he wrote his report in January last. Such promptness is not usual. But admit the fact to be as stated, and what does it prove? Simply that the Lodge violated a solemn edict of its Grand Lodge, and in so doing forfeited its charter. If we had the facts before us, we could better judge of the merits of the case. Our Brother says, this 'visitor, or it appears, presented certificates of his having visited Lodges in Kentucky, Missouri, Wisconsin and Ohio.' The evidence that these were genuine certificates is not given; and we confess it appears to us not a little remarkable, that Lodges in Kentucky and Missouri, both slave holding States, should admit a negro as a visitor among them, even though he did present 'a constitution and By-Laws of a Lodge, deriving authority from the North American Grand Lodge,' a body without a soul, a thing without vitality, and so known to every, even moderately informed Mason in the country. But admit all that is claimed, and what does it prove? Merely that the visitor had so much white blood in him that he was able to impose upon these Lodges, or that the officers of them were exceedingly stupid, and too ignorant of their duty to be longer entrusted with their Charters.

But we have said enough, more than we had intended. The result may be summed up in a few words:

1) In 1846, the Grand Lodge of Illinois, reproved one of its subordinates for admitting a half-blooded Indian as a visitor, and passed a resolution prohibiting, under severe penalty, repetition of the offense.

2) The Grand Lodge of the District of Columbia refused to act on a petition for a Charter for a Lodge in Liberia.

3) The committee of correspondence in the Grand Lodge of New Hampshire, in 1852, thought the resolution of the Grand Lodge of Illinois, too stringent, and went into the discussion of an abstract question, that, in a whole generation to come, will not probably once be brought to a practical test. Thus, giving point and force to the opinion which is rapidly gaining strength, that such reports are productive of as much mischief as good.

4) The Grand Master, under a misapprehension of the acts in the case 'discharged a big gun.'

5) Certain Lodges in Illinois, Kentucky, Missouri, Wisconsin and Ohio, are reputed to have been imposed upon by vagrant clandestine negro Masons; for which piece of folly, they deserved to lose their Charters.

Thus ends the sum and substance of all the grievances of which our good Brother complains. They are certainly not very alarming. And as we cannot discover in them, any 'persistence in pushing the black race into the fraternity,' not yet wherein Grand Lodges 'have been guilty of wrong,' we must be allowed to indulge the opinion, that the evil is not of a magnitude to 'destroy all harmony in the Masonic, as it has in a part of the religious and political world.' If this result is ever to be realized, and God forbid, the surest way to bring it about is to agitate the subject, we have done with it.

(Walkes' Comments) In the "Introductory Remarks" to A Documentary Account of Prince Hall and Other Black Fraternal Orders, by Henry Wilson Coil, Sr., and John MacDuffie Sherman (The Missouri Lodge of Research, 1982), Alphonse Cerza writes under the heading of There is No Color Line in Freemasonry, "There has never been a law in Freemasonry stating that having a white skin is a qualification for membership...In Illinois for over a hundred years the rule has been stated in its law as follows: "Masonry knows no distinction of race or color. It is the mental, moral, and physical qualifications of the men that are to be considered." To say that Mr. Alphonse Cerza doesn't know what he is talking about is putting it mildly!

The incident of the visit to the Illinois Lodge is recorded in Harry E. Davis' History on pages 175-6. "In 1845, Harmon Lodge of Jacksonville, Illinois, filed a formal protest with the Grand Lodge, their grievance being that a colored Mason had been allowed as a visitor in a Chicago Lodge, and that another Lodge, with the approval of the Grand Master, had received petitions for degrees from colored profanes. A committee presenting three Chicago Lodges, LaFayette, Oriental and Apollo, answered the one. A.B. Lewis, a mulatto had been admitted as a visitor on several occasions to several lodges, but was not a member; that Apollo's Lodge had received the petitions of two colored residents, Johnson and Davidson. Action was deferred on these applicants, pending an expression from the Grand Lodge. Later, the committee on petitions was withdrawn. This was in the interest of harmony, as the complaining Lodge (Harmony) belied its name by threatening to secede from the Grand Lodge. The Chicago Lodges, vigorously defended their action as did the Grand Master, W.F. Walker. The Grand Lodge held that the action of the Chicago Lodges was censurable, and tending to create discord, and also because colored men were disqualified by custom and legislative enactment from being recipients of mutual and reciprocal social privileges. A resolution opposing the admission of Negroes or mulattoes into Illinois Lodges was adopted. Anderson B. Lewis, the cause of this incident, was the G.H.P. of the first Grand Chapter (P.H.) formed in Ohio in 1850. He also acted as "Warden" at the organization of Apollo Commandry (White) at Chicago.

Al Cerza, who is a member of the Caucasian Grand Lodge of Illinois, should review a copy of the 2nd Quarter 1981 issue of the Phylaxis magazine, which reproduced a page from the proceedings of the Caucasian Grand Lodge of Illinois, which records "Upon an examination of the proceedings of this Grand Lodge, at its Annual Communication for the year 1846, they find the following expressed opinion of this Grand Lodge upon this subject:

> Resolved, This Grand Lodge is unqualifiedly opposed to the admission of 'negroes or mulattoes' into Lodges under the jurisdiction.

Also in the Davis History on page 85, is discussed the petition of Liberian Masons for a Charter form the Caucasian Grand Lodge of the District of Columbia.

The minutes of this transaction are as follows:

> The R.W. Grand Secretary then laid before the Grand Lodge a communication for Dr. J.W. Lugenbeel, of the Colonization Society in this city, covering a petition from J.J. Roberts, President of the Republic of Liberia, Henry J. Roberts, his brother, Rev. John Day, Rev. Eli W. Stokes, — Harris — Roye, and — Montpelier, citizens of Monrovia in that Republic, praying for a charter for a Lodge to be opened in that place, to be called "Restoration Lodge."
>
> On motion of M.W.P. Grand Master Magruder, the petition was laid on the table, but the motion having been reconsidered and by consent withdrawn, the following resolution offered by P. Master McCalla, was unanimously adopted:

Resolved, that the prayer of the petitioners be rejected.

VOLUME XV (May 1, 1856, page 220)

(Williamson's Comments) This is from the proceedings of the Grand Lodge of Vermont, in which, the Grand Master, Philip C. Tucker, stated he had received: 1) A letter from one Peter C. Smith of Montpelier; 2) A copy of a letter to Smith from J.S. Rock of Boston, Corresponding Grand Secretary of Prince Hall Grand Lodge; 3) A copy of Tucker's letter to Smith; 4) A letter from Winslow Lewis, Grand Master of Massachusetts, upon the correspondence.

While there is nothing to indicate such, one gains the impression that Peter G. Smith must have been a white man who was initiated into a colored Lodge at Boston and was refused admission into a white Lodge in Montpelier, and of course, there was considerable controversy over the status of the Negro brethren, but Winslow Lewis did say, the original Charter of African Lodge had been returned to England for alteration (only a copy being retained by the Lodge) and never returned.

(From the Publication)

NEGRO LODGES

The following correspondence on this subject is so just in the views expressed and so wholly unexceptionable, that we transfer it to our pages, from the recent proceedings of the Grand Lodge of Vermont, as matter of information. The facts stated have been given in previous volumes of this Magazine, but may, nevertheless, be new to many of our present readers:

I lay before the Grand Lodge also, at this time, the following described papers, and deeming them important, ask for them its attentive consideration.

1. A letter to me from Peter G. Smith, of Montpelier, dated September 21, 1855.

2. A copy of a letter from J.S. Rock, of Boston, to Peter G. Smith, dated September 6, 1855, said Rock signing himself as "Corresponding Secretary of Prince Hall Grand Lodge."

3. A copy of a letter from myself to Peter G. Smith, in reply to his letter of September 21, and embracing a reply to the contents of J.S. Rock's letter to him.

4. A letter from M.W. Winslow Lewis, Grand Master of the Grand Lodge of Massachusetts, in reply to a letter addressed to him by me on the subject embraced by the foregoing letters.

The question which these documents immediately involves is not probably doubtful in its charter; but the subject possesses an interest, in view of our present position, and of applications of a like kind which may be made hereafter, which makes it our duty to meet it with prudence and wisdom. There are other questions obviously related to the present one, which are glimmering in the distance, and the agitation of which may perhaps be foreshown by this. Although "sufficient for the day is the evil thereof," it is certainly not unwise to anticipate and be prepared for the future.

I have endeavored to place the present question upon its plain and simple merits, and, have, in my letter to Mr. Smith, entered into it more at large than I should have done, had I not been desirous of having it thoroughly understood by all the Brethren of this Masonic jurisdiction. I have contended, and I believe, have established the position, that the bodies of colored men in Boston, claiming to be regular Masonic Lodges, are illegitimate, spurious and clandestine, and that, consequently, no man receiving the degrees in them, whether white or colored, can be recognized as a regular Mason or received as such into any regular Lodges of Masons. With these views, however innocently or ignorantly Mr. Smith may have acted, in becoming a member of one of those bodies, my plain duty left me no other course than to instruct Aurora Lodge not to receive him as a Mason.

Following is the correspondence referred to in the foregoing:

Montpelier, September 21, 1855

Mr. P.C. Tucker

Sir:

I went to Boston last June and joined a Lodge of Masons. When I returned to Montpelier, I asked for a seat in the Lodge and was refused on the ground that it was said to be a clandestine Lodge. I then wrote back to Boston, not wishing to be imposed upon, and got the letter enclosed. I showed it to Mr. Washburn of Montpelier, and he told me what you had said to him and wished me to write to you, and you would give me the facts in the case. Sir, you will oblige me by answering this, and returning the letters.

Peter G. Smith

Copies of the letters enclosed by me, Peter G. Smith, of Montpelier, Vermont and received by me September 22, 1855.

No. 60 South Street,

Boston, September 7, 1855, A.L. 5855

Peter G. Smith, Esq.,

My Dear Sir and Brother — Yours bearing date August 14, came duly to hand. You say that the Grand Master of Vermont, says that the colored Masons had their Charter taken from them, and that they are now working without a Charter. We reply that the charge is no doubt innocent, but it is nevertheless false from beginning to end. The original Charter is now in our possession, and always has been, and we worked under it until some time after the war between this country and Great Britain, when the colored Masons had a Convention and declared themselves independent, the same as the whites had already done before. This was done on account of the difficulties of making the returns to the mother country. There has always been the best feeling, and our Brethren all visit the Lodges, not only in England, but <u>in all parts of the world</u>.

If the Grand Master of Vermont wishes any more light we are prepared to give it to him; or if he has a curiosity, he can see the original Charter.

Yours fraternally,

J.S. Rock

Corresponding Secretary of Prince Hall Grand Lodge

Copy of letter from Philip C. Tucker, Grand Master, to Peter G. Smith:

Vergennes, September 22, 1855

Mr. Peter G. Smith, Montpelier, Sir:

I received yours of yesterday, enclosing a letter to you from Mr. J.S. Rock of Boston this morning.

As to the Lodge of colored men existing in Boston, calling itself "Prince Hall Grand Lodge," and such Lodges as acknowledge its jurisdiction, I have to say that my understanding on the subject is this:

I suppose it to be true, that on the 20th day of September, 1784, a Charter for a Master's Lodge was granted to Prince Hall and others, under the authority of the Grand Lodge of England, and that the Lodge thus chartered, bore the name of "African Lodge, No. 459," and was located at Boston. If any other Charter was ever granted, at any other time, by the Grand Lodge of England or any other Grand Lodge, to the colored persons of that city, it has never come to my knowledge.

I suppose it to be also true, that African Lodge, No. 459, did not continue its connection for many years with the Grand Lodge of England, and that its registration was stricken from the rolls of that Grand Lodge more than fifty years ago.

I suppose it further to be also true, that this Lodge, No. 459, and all others which have originated from it, have always held themselves aloof from, and have always refused to acknowledge any allegiance to, the Grand Lodge of the Commonwealth of Massachusetts.

I also further suppose to be true, that on the 18th day of June, 1827, this same Lodge, No. 459, issued a declaration, and had it published in some of the Boston papers, signed by John T. Hilton, Thomas Dalton, Lewis York, Jr., and J.H. Purrow, (claiming to be Master, Wardens and Secretary thereof), which declaration contained the following language: "We publicly declare ourselves free and independent of any Lodge from this day, and we will not be tributary or governed by any Lodge than that of our own."

And I still further suppose it to be true, that in the month of July, 1845, R.W. Charles

W. Montpelier, the Grand Secretary of the Grand Lodge of Massachusetts, had a personal interview with Mr. Hilton, then Master of this same Lodge, No. 459, at which interview Mr. Hilton said, that they (the members of said Lodge), were entirely independent of all white Lodges, asked no favors of them, and would have nothing to do with them; nor would they admit a white Mason, if he should present himself as a visitor.

All three things are of record, and cannot, I think, be truthfully denied in any quarter. From them I form the following opinions:

1. Even if a Charter for a subordinate Lodge, to be located within the United States, could be lawfully granted by the Grand Lodge of England, after the close of the American Revolution, and if such Charter could be lawfully recognized by the American Lodge, its vitality would necessarily expire when the grantor substantially revoked the grant by striking it from its records and thus disavowing all connection with the grantee.

2. That the mere retention of a Charter, after its legal revocation, cannot preserve or retain any right, power or authority, in the original grantees or their successors, where the right to revoke is reserved, as it always is in all Grand Lodges, in the grantor.

3. Even if African Lodge, No. 459, had a lawful Masonic existence June 18, 1847, the declaration of that date was both unmasonic and revolutionary, and places that body as effectually beyond recognition by either the Grand Lodge of Massachusetts or any other Grand Lodges in the United States, as was the French Lodge of Virginia, or are the German Lodges of New York.

4. Had African Lodge, No. 459, been in all things a lawful Lodge, after the declaration of its first officer of July, 1845, that "it would not admit a white Mason if he should present himself as a visitor," it would have been both humiliating and degrading to have allowed the doors of the white Lodges to stand open for reciprocity of courtesies which were thus gratuitously and roughly declared inadmissible, in advance of any request, offer, or wish to establish them.

I have the highest Masonic authority in Massachusetts for denying that "the Brethren " of the Lodge in question "all visit the Lodges," so far as the Lodges of Massachusetts are concerned. A Past Grand Master of the Grand Lodge of that Commonwealth, writing at Boston in 1848, says: — "There are no Lodges of colored Masons in this city or any other part of the United States, that are recognized and acknowledged by the Grand Lodge of Massachusetts, or, to our knowledge, by any other regularly constituted Grand Lodge in this country. It (the African Lodge) was never recognized by the Grand Lodge of this State, nor has there ever been any Masonic intercourse between the two Bodies." The same Brother, writing at the same place in 1846, says, referring to that Lodge: "Applications have several times been made by its members for admission to our Lodges, but they have generally, if not always, been refused." Again, he says, "That the course of our Grand Lodge in reference to African Lodge, is not the result of prejudice, it is only necessary for me to say, that within the last month, a colored Brother from England has visited, and been kindly received in one of our city Lodges."

I believe I am correct in stating, that the two following propositions are recognized as sound Masonic law in this country.

1. That no Grand Lodge of any State can regularly recognize a Subordinate Lodge existing in another State, or its members, until such Subordinate Lodge is recognized by the Grand Lodge of the State in which it exists.

2. That no Grand Lodge, either in these United States, or any other country, can legally establish a Subordinate Lodge in any other State where a regularly constituted Grand Lodge exists.

From these views you will readily perceive why the Masonry of the United States does not and cannot recognize either "Prince Hall Grand Lodge," or its Subordinates, or their members, as regular. To our understanding, the whole of these organizations are irregular and unmasonic, and exist adverse to Masonic regulations and law. If, as Mr. Rock asserts, members of these bodies are admitted to "visit Lodges in England and all parts of the world," that admission probably rises from the fact, that the history and Masonic positions of these bodies are not as well understood elsewhere as they are in the United States.

Mr. Rock expresses an inclination to "give the Grand Master of Vermont more light" on this subject. As he signed himself "Corresponding Secretary of Prince Hall Grand Lodge," I suppose him to possess all the "light" which the subject has in it; and whatever that light may be able to reflect upon me, of the truth of the past or present, will always receive the respectful attention it may deserve, from,

Your obedient servant.

Philip C. Tucker

Grand Master of the Grand Lodge of Vermont

P.S. I return Mr. Rock's letter, according to your request.

Office of the Grand Master of the Grand Lodge of Massachusetts.

Boston, October 3, 1855.

M.W. Philip C. Tucker, Grand Master of the Grand Lodge of Vermont.

Dear Sir and Brother:

In reply to yours of the 26th, I can only re-affirm all that you have stated, that the Grand Lodge of this State does not recognize the "Prince Hall Grand Lodge" or any other Lodge of colored Masons have ever visited or would be allowed to visit our Lodges. No white Masons to my knowledge ever entered a black lodge. So far as I have ascertained, the blacks have once possessed a Charter from England, which Charter (a copy being taken) was returned to its source for alteration, and was never sent back to this country, and the copy of the aforesaid is all the blacks now have.

But I shall endeavor to see that Instrument, and will then notify you of the facts, etc. Trusting to have at some time the honor of a personal interview, I am, very truly and,

Fraternally yours,

Winslow Lewis, Grand Master

(Walkes' Comments)

This is a perfect example why Caucasians should not be allowed to write anything about Blacks, as a rule they do not know what they are talking about, and in the second, they are known not to be too truthful.

VOLUME XVIII (June 1, 1859, page 247)

(Williamson's Comments)

De Molay Commandery of Knights Templar of Boston visited Richmond Encampment No. 2, at Richmond, Virginia, and in a portion of the account of that visit, the following story:

Purchase of a Slave

It will perhaps surprise our Boston people to learn that one of the De Molays has bought a slave since he came here. Yet such is the fact. The circumstances are these: A colored woman in Boston some years ago lost her husband who was formerly a slave, and who left her quite a snug sum of money. She married again and her second husband also died. She has learned recently that a brother of her first husband was held as a slave in this city, and that he could be bought for $800. She placed that amount in the hands of a Sir Knight with instructions to buy the man. He has seen the master and completed the purchase. It is understood that she, for whom the purchase was made, intends to bind the captive in hymen's chains, when he shall have become acclimated to our New England soil.

(Walkes' Comments)

The short text from the publication is quite interesting. It is well known however, that many Caucasian Freemasons were deeply involved in the slave trade. One such celebrated Freemason was George Washington. Of course, it is also known that slave-owners were kidnappers, and in-fact, criminals.

Therefore the Grand Lodges that supported them were in reality giving aid and comfort to criminals, and therefore at that very instant stopped being Masonic and placed itself outside of the pale of Freemasonry. As I had noted in Black Square & Compass and again in the Prince Hall Masonic Quiz Book, from the letter of Mahatma Gandhi to Bro. W.E.B. DuBois "There is no dishonor in being slaves. There is dishonor in being slave-owners."

VOLUME XVIII (September 1, 1859, page 329)

(Williamson's Comments)

This carries an account of the laying of the cornerstone of the Pilgrim Monument at Plymouth and the following statement appears in the account on page above and it reads as follows:

> "After the benediction the procession was reformed and proceeded to dinner, which was spread by the celebrated caterer J.B. Smith, of Boston, under a mammoth tent, capable of holding about three thousand persons, and which we nearly filled on the present occasion."

(Walkes Comments)

Harold Van Buren Voorhis' Negro Masonry in the United States, pages 106-7, gives us a brief history on J.B. Smith; under Chapter 9 "Negro Masons in other White Lodges after 1870":

> St. Andrew's Lodge, Boston, Massachusetts — Joshua Bowen Smith, a Negro, was born in Coatsville, Pennsylvania, on November 3, 1813, and came North in 1836 and settled in Cambridge, Massachusetts. He was Entered on October 10, 1867, Passed on November 14, and Raised on December 12 in St. Andrew's Lodge. In those days it was the custom for lodges to make Masons and consider their application for membership separately. Brother Smith did not affiliate with St. Andrew's Lodge but on January 16, 1872, he affiliated with Adelphi Lodge, South Boston. He was a very renowned caterer at the time. He became Warden of his Lodge and thus a member of the Grand Lodge of Massachusetts during his term of office. He represented the City of Cambridge in the State Legislature in 1873 and 1874.
>
> Brother Smith was made a Royal Arch Mason in St. Matthews Royal Arch Chapter, South Boston, on June 14, 1869. He was Knighted in St. Omer Commandery, K.T., South Boston, November 15, 1869.
>
> In the Ancient and Accepted Scottish Rite, Brother Smith was given the degrees from the 4th to the 14th, on May 21, 1869, in Boston Lodge of Perfection, by Communication. He received the 17th and 18th degrees in full ceremonial form on the same date in Mt. Olivet Chapter of the Rose Croix, Boston. These dates are taken directly from the minute books of the two bodies. There are no exact records of this period for Boston Council, Princes of Jerusalem, but he must have had the 15th and 16th degrees communicated to him in that Council the same night or he would not have been able to take the degrees in the Chapter without them. The records of the Supreme Council show that he was made a 32nd Degree Mason on the same date in Boston Sovereign Consistory and his name is listed in the Proceedings of the Supreme Council in the report of the Deputy. A roster of members of Massachusetts Consistory (a combination of Boston, DeWitt Clinton and Massachusetts Consistories) dated 1877, shows him listed as a member.
>
> There is an extended Memorial of him in the records of Boston Lodge of Perfection, dated November 24, 1879. He had died July 5, 1879.
>
> This is the only record which shows a Negro in a white Chapter, Commandery and Consistory. References to him are to be found in the Boston newspapers on

December 1, 1867 and in The Grand Lodge of St. Andrew and the Massachusetts Grand Lodge, 1870.

VOLUME XIX (December 1, 1859, page 33)

(Williamson's Comments)

This carries the caption of "Grand Lodge of Hamburg and African Lodges," and speaks of the action of the German Grand Body in its recognition of Prince Hall jurisdictions over here, which likewise had difficulty with New York because of the formation of a Lodge in New York City, Pythagoras No. 86, which severed its allegiance with New York, and became identified with the Hamburg body, over the question of color, but this particular article is about folks of color.

(From the Publication)

Grand Lodge of Hamburg and African Lodges

We give below an interesting and ably drawn report on the subject of colored Masons and African Lodges, from the proceedings of the Grand Lodge of Hamburg, on May 6, 1858, together with the comments thereon by the committee of correspondence of the Grand Lodge of New York. It presents the strongest argument on the negro-side of the question we have met with, though the writer of the report was manifestly either not well informed or was wholly indifferent to the relations which the colored race in this country sustain to the white population. In England, or Holland, or wherever else the social equality of the races is recognized, the argument would be irresistible. But no such equality is here admitted; or at least not to any very considerable extent. The black is here held to be the inferior race, and qualified neither by nature or habits to become the companion and equal of the white man. Without stopping to inquire whether this be just or otherwise, it may be safely assumed that it is the fixed and unalterable sentiment of the people of this country; and all attempts to change it — to debase the white or to elevate the black race to a common level of equality, are as futile as would be an attempt to change any fixed law of nature. The thing can never be accomplished through any agency less powerful than the hand of Him who created all races of men. Call it prejudice or anything else, the fact is undeniable and unalterable. Were it expedient, therefore, to authorize the establishment of colored Lodges among us — even in the Northern States, where the black race may be supposed to be as favorably considered as elsewhere in the country — there never could be any common sympathy or fraternal brethren. They would be strangers to each other, though members of the same household. It is so in all the relations of society — in business, in schools, in churches, in religion. The two races

are not, and cannot be brought together in equality anywhere, or under any circumstances, whether social, political, masonic, or religious. And if any of our Brethren in this country or elsewhere have succeeded in reasoning it to a consummation, by removing the barriers to their admission and equality in our Lodges, we beg to suggest, in all frankness, and with due respect for their philanthropic sympathies, that the sooner they give up such expectation, the better it will be for all the parties interested.

The propriety of recognizing the so called colored Lodges in this country, and which, it should appear, have petitioned the Grand Lodge of Hamburg for recognition, is a matter which is at once set at rest by the fact that all such Lodges, if they exist at all (as they doubtless do, and in considerable numbers), are unlawful, and therefore unrecognizable bodies. There is not a masonically lawful Lodge of colored Masons in the United States, nor are there probably colored Masons enough in the country to form one, — Masons we mean, of course, who have been regularly admitted to the Institution according to the recognized forms and laws of Masonry. There are therefore no colored Lodges, and with the exception of a very few colored men, who have been made Masons in foreign countries, no colored Masons, which the Grand Lodge of Hamburg, nor any other Grand Lodge in Europe, can recognize as Masonic bodies, without trampling under foot, not only their own solemn engagements, but those fundamental laws which underlie the whole superstructure of Masonry. The question of recognition therefore, as applied to the so-called colored Lodges in this country, is not a debatable one. It is not one that any Grand Lodge, having the facts presumed that the Grand Lodge of Hamburg, when more correctly informed as to the true condition of the case, will at once dismiss the subject. The report, above referred to, is as follows:

> "The Grand Lodge of Hamburg, beg leave to submit to the consideration of those sister Grand Lodges in Europe, more intimately connected with a matter of general importance, requesting them to report their opinion on what action in relation thereto, might be necessary to be taken, and which at the same time might be calculated to meet the approbation of a majority of them.
>
> There exists in some of the States of North America, besides the Lodges at Hayti, many independent Lodges of colored people, (negroes, mulattoes, etc.) as for instance, in Massachusetts, New York, Pennsylvania, Ohio, New Jersey, Maryland, etc. They are united under Grand Lodges under the jurisdiction of a National Grand Lodge of America. We know little about them, because they are declared by the North American Grand Lodges as clandestine Lodges, and all Masonic intercourse with them is strictly forbidden. Their origin is unknown. The African Lodge at Boston, insists upon having obtained its charter from the Grand Lodge of England, that is, however, doubtful. According to an assertion of some of our German brethren, who have, free from prejudice, visited negro Lodges in New

York, they could find nothing tending to prevent them from pronouncing these Lodges just and perfect. In North America, however, in the land of boasted liberty, a negro or mulatto, in short, any person in whose veins a single drop of colored blood runs — be he twice as righteous, honest, well-educated, talented and scientific, is considered an outcast, and all intercourse with such person is regarded as a disgrace. The prejudice against colored people, even in those States not counted as slave States, and where none of but free negroes live, as for instance in the State of New York, is of such a nature, that no white person would sit down with a negro at the same table, or travel with one in the same stage. That even our American brethren are not free from this prejudice, is a fact well known and deeply to be regretted. In the transactions of the Grand Lodge of New York (Willard), for 1855, the question whether colored persons could be admitted as Masons, was regarded as a monstrous proposition, and unworthy of discussion.

At the Masonic Convention in Paris, in 1855, Bro. Cummings, Representative of Washington, insinuated that the European Lodges in consideration of the condition in America, might be induced not to admit negroes. This insinuation was, however, rejected. Under these prejudicial circumstances on the part of the North American Grand Lodges, it is impossible to avoid the conclusion that colored Lodges and colored Grand Lodges never will be recognized by them. But are the Grand Lodges of Europe, where such prejudices are unknown, thereby bound to deny the legitimacy of a great number of otherwise just and lawful Lodges, and to refuse their brethren admittance into our Lodges because they are of a darker race? The fact that a Grand Lodge of a negro State — that of Hyati, with its Subordinates — has been recognized by most of the European Grand Lodges, as a legal Grand Lodge, and that its representative at the Masonic Convention at Paris has been accredited, and furthermore and in particular, the fact that this Grand Lodge is enumerated as such on the list of Prussian Grand Lodges, is sufficient proof that such a prejudice has no existence in European Grand Lodges. The Grand Lodge of another negro State, that of the Republic of Liberia in Africa, although too young yet and too little known, may in the course of time, rely upon being recognized by the European Grand Lodges as well as that of Hayti. As to the Grand Lodges and their Subordinates of colored people, the North American Grand Lodges might appeal to a monopoly, according to which only one Grand Lodge can legally exist in one and the same State; and no Lodge can legally exist in such State without the sanction of the Grand Lodge thereof. This monopoly has been created by common consent, and is not founded, for instance, in Prussia, on a demand of the government.

The Grand Lodge of Hamburg, in consequence of having been regardless of this monopoly, as far as it concerns German Lodges, came in conflict with them. On this ground, the right of discussing the propriety of such monopoly might, to the

Grand Lodge of Hamburg, be denied; but here it must be premised that this action of the Grand Lodge of Hamburg has only reference to such Lodges, which, if they had been disposed to join the Grand Lodge of the State, would, undoubtedly, have been rejected by the same on the supposition that the members of such Lodges were unfit for reception. When American Lodges, in respect to a general prejudice prevailing there, deem it proper to reject colored persons, when they refuse members of colored Lodges admittance, forbidding at the same time all Masonic intercourse with them, they may, politically, be in the right, but not masonically, and cannot expect European Lodges to agree with them on this point. The connection of Europe with other parts of the world, increasing from year to year, demands a discussion of this question, which were long, may be submitted to the consideration of each European Lodge, in particular to Lodges in seaports and in Germany, but to the Lodges at Hamburg. The Grand Lodge of Hamburg will, at its next convention, make this question the topic of deliberation, relying thereby upon the support of its sister Grand Lodges, desiring them to communicate their views and intentions in respect to the recognition of the Grand Lodge of the Republic of Liberia in Africa, but in particular in respect to the Lodges and Grand Lodges of colored people, pronounced by the American Grand Lodges to be clandestine."

There are some features of this report that are very singular, and would be unaccountable but for the fact that a Mason from Hamburg is unknown in America and he will continue to be a stranger in this land of charities and Masonic benevolence so long as that unwise body on the continent of Europe, which bears that name, shall persist in the support and countenance of its Subordinates in this jurisdiction. Speaking of the negro "Lodges" this report says:

"Their origin is unknown. The African Lodge at Boston insists upon having obtained its charter from the Grand Lodge of England; this is however, doubtful. According to an assertion of some of our German Brethren, who have free of prejudice, visited negro Lodges in New York, they could find nothing tending to prevent them to pronounce these Lodges just and perfect."

In the first place, has the Grand Lodge of Hamburg ever been appealed to by those negro Lodges to recognize them? Not at all; Hamburg will not so pretend. What business then, has that body to be meddling with this matter? And more than three thousand miles away! None whatever. Do they know of the rejection of a colored individual by one of our Lodges? Do they know, or have they been informed of the exclusion of a single member of a "colored Lodge" from the doors of a white man's Lodge? Has it been intimated to Hamburg, that all intercourse with colored Masons have been forbidden? We present these questions only to show the inconsistency of the pretensions of Hamburg. And these are the grounds upon which it goes out to the Grand Lodges of Europe with an earnest appeal for the recognition of colored Lodges in this country. And yet, strange as it may appear, there is not the slightest proof — there is not the shadow of evidence, that we are obnoxious to one of these charges. And yet, Hamburg asks the Grand Lodges of Europe to recognize these bodies, when it declares their origin is "unknown" and their pretensions "doubtful." Some of the "German Brethren" have visited these negro Lodges in New York! We respectfully submit that the Grand Lodge of Hamburg is mistaken in this particular. No German Brother has ever visited one of these Lodges. Such a thing cannot be done — for the moment a Mason enters the portals of such a body in New York, in character of a Mason, his panoply of a "Brother" departs from him. There may be, and doubtless have been, white persons, perhaps Germans, who have visited negro assemblages which were called by the negroes themselves "Masonic Lodges," but these assemblages bear about the same affinity to a Masonic Lodge that a negro clambake would bear to the Diet of Worms! None but irregular, clandestine or expelled Masons visit these bodies of Masons; the Mason in good standing who should visit one of these bodies would subject himself to expulsion, and would be expelled as soon as the subject could be brought before his Lodge — not so much because the body is made up of colored men, though this would cause a suspicion of his orthodoxy, but because there is not and never has been a negro Lodge of Masons in the State of New York, deriving authority from a regular Grand Lodge. A moment's reflection will convince any Mason that such a body cannot be visited without a violation of the most solemn obligations.

The Grand Lodge of Europe is supposed to be without prejudice to the colored race, and is, therefore, asked to recognize these bodies! Extravagant credulity! Can it be possible that Hamburg believes the other Grand Lodges of Europe will recognize negro Lodges and Grand Lodges solely because their members have dark skins? This idea presupposes any affection for the colored race on the part of the European Grand Lodges, which would trample upon Masonic obligations to be gratified. Those bodies cannot commit, nor permit their members to commit so great a crime. There must be some other evidence furnished those Grand Lodges of the regularity of these negro Lodges before they will acknowledge them and when they come to seek for this evidence, it will be entirely wanting.

(Walkes' Comments)

One can see the "sickness" of American Freemasonry in the above. Harry E. Davis covers this briefly on page 162 of his history. He writes,

> "Pythagoras Lodge No. 1 of Brooklyn, New York, subordinate to the Grand Lodge of Hamburg, as early as 1847, admitted colored visitors and returned such visits, and even adopted a resolution to that effect, although it refrained from conferring degrees upon colored men. It was this Lodge which later was the subject of a bitter

controversy between the Grand Lodges of Hamburg and New York over territorial question. The refusal to confer degrees was temporary, the Lodge carefully refraining from making a final commitment on this point. In 1853, members of eleven German Lodges in New York assembled to consider establishing a Grand Lodge, pronounced in favor of the admission of colored Masons from regular lodges. It is interesting to observe that while New York assailed the sympathetic attitude of Germany toward colored Masons, yet a few years previously, this same Grand Lodge took issue with the Germans because of their attitude in prescribing the initiation of Jews.

The complete history of the above is fully recorded in "Masonic Truths: A Letter and a Document" by Arthur A. Schomburg, Grand Secretary of the Prince Hall Grand Lodge of New York. Perhaps the Lux e Tenebris might consider republishing this important pamphlet in its "Document" section one day.

VOLUME XIX (February 1, 1860, page 122)

(Williamson's Comments)

This is a transcript of the Charter issued to African Lodge No. 459, in 1784.

(From the Publication)

The following is a copy of the Charter procured of the Grand Master of England, by Capt. James Scott of Boston, for Prince Hall and his associates, in 1784, and under which a Lodge of colored Masons was in that year formed in this city. It is proper to add that the Lodge was many years stricken from the roll of the Grand Lodge of England, and that it has never been recognized as a regular body by the Grand Lodge of this Commonwealth.

(Walkes' Comments)

Following the above introduction, is the entire Warrant of African Lodge No. 459. We are all acquainted with it, and there is no need to reproduce it here. What editor Montpelier has failed to record is that when the two rival Grand Lodges in England consolidated in 1813, all of the Lodges on the registers of both jurisdictions in the United States and which had not contributed to the Grand Charity Fund (of the 1717 body at least), were erased; but according to Caucasian American Freemasonry, the erasure appears to have affected only African Lodge. Isn't that rather strange?

There were 28 Lodges in the United States which were dropped at the time of the Union (African Lodge excluded), and of that number, eight are still known to be working at this date. So the questions must be asked if the erasure did not affect those eight Lodges, in what form or manner did it affect African Lodge differently?

VOLUME XIX (May 1, 1860, page 215)

(Williamson's Comments)

About three pages are devoted to further discussion of the Grand Lodge of Hamburg and the colored grand bodies in several states.

VOLUME XX (April 1, 1861, page 190)

(Williamson's Comments)

The following has been transcribed under the caption of "Sham Introduction of Negroes to the Gridiron" and it reads,

> Joseph Gundy, a negro, was recently arrested in New York on a charge of having swindled nine South Carolinian negroes out of $1.50 each. The Southern importations recently arrived in that city, and meeting Gundy, consulted with him on the propriety of going to Hyati. Gundy thought that if they could join the Freemasons they could do well enough in New York, and kindly offered to initiate them into the mysteries of that Order for the frivoling sum of $1.50 each. The negroes produced the fee and Gundy took them to his house on Jersey Street, where they were put through a peculiar formula of grips and heated irons and pronounced Freemasons. Whether the iron was too hot or the grip too strong does not appear, but one of the negroes, fancying that all was not right, went to the Rev. Mr. Thompsons, a colored minister, and after unfolding the mysteries into which he had been inducted, learned that he and his companions had been swindled and thereupon caused the arrest of Gundy. On searching the prisoner's house, the officers found a magazine of paraphernalia pertaining to various secret orders, such as the Odd Fellows, Order of Ancient Romans, Daughters of Ruth, Sons of Malta, Ancient Hibernians, and the P.A. Association.

(Walkes' Comments)

We have some Black bogus organizations claiming to be Masonic that are doing the same thing today.

VOLUME XX (August 1, 1861, page 317)

(Williamson's Comments)

Under the title of "Pennsylvania on the Negro and Hamburg Question" there is more discussion about the subject, and reference is made to a pamphlet bearing the title of "Documents Respecting the Controversy between the Grand Lodges of Hamburg and New York" published by the Masonic Historical Society at Brooklyn, New York.

The above pamphlet contains the accurate material under that title and a copy of the same can be found in the Williamson's Collection on Negro Masonry in the New York Public Library. The proceedings of the Grand Lodge of New York about that period carries similar matter under the same title but the text has been changed in several instances in order to sustain its point of view.

(From the Publication)

From the Report of the Committee on Foreign Correspondence of the Grand Lodge of Pennsylvania, published by authority, we learn the following in relation to the "Documents Respecting the Controversy between the Grand Lodges of Hamburg and New York," published by the Masonic Historical Society in Brooklyn.

We do not recognize these "documents" as Masonic, or coming within that class of publications which are entitled to be Masonically considered by this Grand Lodge. They are not authorized by any Grand Lodges with which the Grand Lodge of Pennsylvania is in correspondence. This might be all that is necessary to be said concerning them. We desire, however, to remark that we do not recognize any convocation of negroes or "colored men," whatever, denominated as "Free and Accepted Ancient York Masons." We do not recognize any proceedings, acts or institution of such persons, as entitled to Masonic attention. As well might we be called upon to notice a meeting of persons, who have no other Masonic right to confraternity with Masons, than their self-styled and unauthorized Masonic name. There is but one source of Masonic life, and but one mode of Masonic investiture. There is but one door into the true Masonic fold, and he that seeks to enter by any opening fails in his purposes. There is but one light which enlightens the Masonic eye, and heart, and mind, and he who professes to have that light, from elsewhere than a temple dedicated to true Masonry, is an impostor. We do not recognize colored persons as Masons, and hence they are not entitled to any of the rights and privileges of Masons. This forecloses any discussion on the so-called controversy between these Grand Lodges. We are equally decided and uncompromising on the questions of the right of any R.W. Grand Lodge to grant a Charter for a subordinate Lodge within the Masonic jurisdiction of an existing, recognized Grand Lodge. It is worthy of the consideration of the R.W. Grand Lodges of the United States how far they will submit to any such violation of their sovereign authority. However, any of them may feel disposed to question the want of energetic and prompt action of the Grand Lodge of Pennsylvania on subjects of minor Masonic importance, on this they will acknowledge she will not be "slow" to express her opinions and to act. This is the first time Pennsylvania has spoken on this controversy and there is no mistaking her language.

(Walkes' Comments)

I have a photocopy of the pamphlet referred to by Montpelier. The pamphlet has two parts, which are:

1. On the exclusive Territorial Jurisdiction of Grand Lodges.

2. On the inquiry concerning the Regularity of colored Lodges.

While Montpelier rants that, "we do not recognize these 'documents' as Masonic, or coming within that class of publication which are entitled to be Masonically considered by this Grand Lodge, etc." The pamphlet was printed by members of the New York Lodges of the Grand Lodge of Hamburg.

Its introduction is hereby printed:

INTRODUCTION

In accordance with the resolutions of the "Masonic Historical Society in Brooklyn, (Engbund New York)" the following documents are submitted to the inspection and judgment of the Masonic World. They show the acts of the Grand Lodge of Hamburg relative to the question of Exclusive Territorial Jurisdiction of Grand Lodges, and also relative to an Inquiry concerning the Regularity of Colored Lodges, so called, which it had become necessary for the Grand Lodges of Hamburg to make, on account of applications for recognition, brought directly before that Grand Body, in behalf of a colored Lodge in Liberia.

The acts of Hamburg have been represented in the Report of the Committee on Foreign Correspondence of the Grand Lodge of New York, to that Grand Body, at the communication of June 1859, in such a manner as to convey erroneous impressions to masons not familiar with the actual occurrences; and the criticisms embodied in that report are as harsh and unbrotherly as they are unjust in view of the true facts.

The press, both masonic and public, caught up the subject at the time, and published misrepresentations concerning the Grand Lodge of Hamburg, calculated to throw odium on a Grand Body, standing high in the estimation of all European Grand Lodges, and second to no Grand Body in the world in its devotion to the true principles of Freemasonry.

The undersigned, in his capacity of W.M. of one of the daughter Lodges of Hamburg, felt it incumbent upon him, then, to transmit to the Masonic Mirror & Keystone, published in Philadelphia, and the New York Courier, extracts from the Minutes of the Grand Lodge of Hamburg, showing the injustice of these attacks, and to ask for them the same publicity which had been given to the latter.

Both these periodicals refused to accede to his request, which the entire world of letters must concede to have been fair and proper. An example has thus been given, by leading masons, of denying a hearing to a party attacked. It is fit that this fact should be generally known among masons. It shows how far passion and prejudice can blunt the sense of justice and fairness, which is a constituent of every human heart; and whose development and refinement is one of the noblest tasks of Freemasonry. It will, perhaps incline hundreds of honorable masons to an attentive perusal of the documents here-in-after published, who have perhaps, until now, taken no particular interest in the question at issue between the Grand Lodges of Hamburg and New York. For the love of fair play is deeply rooted in the American heart, and conduct like that of the editors alluded to is calculated to provoke censure from every honest man, much more from every true Freemason.

The Report of the Committee on Foreign Correspondence being, to a large extent, based upon reports of the Representative of the Grand Lodge of New York with the Grand Lodge of Saxony, Br. von Mensch, the undersigned, also felt impelled to address, to the latter, an elaborate communication, with the view of convincing him of the errors into which he had been led by his official zeal, in behalf of the Grand Body, which he represents.

The reply of Br. von Mensch to this communication shows that the latter had not entirely failed of its effect. That W. Br. had already protested in a letter to the Grand Secretary Br. Austin, and in this reply to the undersigned, also protests against the manner in which it reports to the Grand Lodge of Saxony, had been used and distorted by the Committee on Foreign Correspondence. All these documents, being necessary elements of a full history of the controversy existing between the Grand Lodges, have been deposited by the undersigned, in the Archives of the Masonic Historical Society, whose president he has the honor to be, and are now published, by the resolution of that society, and at its expense, for the purpose of diffusing correct historical information on a topic of more than ordinary interest to American Freemasons, and especially to those of the State of New York.

It is hoped that a full understanding of the facts bearing upon the controversy will have a tendency to correct the erroneous impressions now prevailing with grand numbers of masons, respecting the views entertained and the position assumed by the Grand Lodge of Hamburg, and concerning the regularity and fair masonic standing of its daughter Lodges in this state, Pythagoras No. 1 and Franklin No. 2.

It is also hoped that peace and harmony may finally result from this elucidation and that elements long estranged may, by degrees, be led back to that fraternal concord which should ever link heart to heart through the entire chain of masons, the world over.

Brooklyn, June 1860

R. Barthelmes,

PRESIDENT, MAS. HISTORICAL SOCIETY

(Engbund New York)

What the President of the Masonic Historical Society learned is something that we Prince Hall Freemasons have ever known, that American Caucasian Freemasons are not above misrepresentation of facts and not above book burning to destroy light when that subject is about Prince Hall Freemasonry. I had noted in Part VII in my book, Black Square and Compass, page 115, that the actions of the New York Caucasian Grand Lodge was "considered by this writer as one of the most shameful incidents in Masonic history."

The President of the Masonic Historical Society also noted that the Grand Lodge of Hamburg was refused space to defend itself in the Masonic and public press, and again we Prince Hall Freemasons know that well. I recorded the same in my book under the title of "Niggerdom in Regalia." Perhaps one day, one of our Masonic writers will record the events that took place between the two Masonic powers and publish it within the pages of Lux E Tenebris.

VOLUME XXI (March 1, 1862, page 155)

(Williamson's Comments)

Under "Colored Lodges" there is the usual prejudiced manner along with a transcript of the African Lodge Charter, and was reproduced from an issue of The New York Sunday Courier.

(From the Publication)

But little is known among the regular Fraternity in the United States of the condition of Freemasonry among the negroes, and yet, during the week which closed the year 1861, a so-called Grand Lodge of that persuasion was held in the city of New York, and election had, by which some of the sons of "Ham" were elected to the rank of Grand Dignitaries, with all the high-sounding titles in which that imitative race takes so great a pride.

These "colored brudders" have, on more occasion than one, in years gone by, published their list of dignitaries in the columns of our contemporaries, and, probably with the desire of receiving the benefit of our extended Masonic circulation, this year honored us with their notice but, though deeply sensible of the intended honor, we most respectfully declined to be the medium of communication between them and the regular constituted Fraternities in the United States.

While we have every desire to promote the interest of genuine Freemasonry, we have no inclination to give prominence to that which is bastard and spurious, and without designing any affront to the "sons of Africa" we cannot consent, directly and indirectly, to elevate them to an equality with the white or dominant race in our columns.

The existence of these so-called Masonic lodges among the blacks has never been recognized by any Grand Lodge of Freemasons in the United States. Their origin was not in accordance with the laws of the Institution, and it is doubtful whether their continuance is not, from the material of which they are in part at least said to be composed, a direct infraction of that Ancient law which requires of all candidates for initiation into the mysteries of the Society to be "freeborn" or "no bondmen."

The authority under which these negro Lodges claim to derive their power is of itself, a sufficient evidence of their irregularity; and, in order that our readers may be thoroughly posted on the subject, we will give a verbatim copy of the document upon the strength of which they have based their organization.

HERE FOLLOWS THE WARRANT OF 459

Under such an authority as the above is it that the colored population have ventured to establish a National Grand Lodge, which in turn, grants Warrants to State Grand Lodges, and these latter to Subordinate Lodges.

The basis upon which the negroes have raised their superstructure according to the laws which prevail among Masons, especially in the U.S., is factually defective, and their work consequently illegitimate. In the first place, the Grand Lodge of England had no right, in 1784, to establish a Lodge in Boston, as there was a Grand Lodge, exercising authority, established there, for the State of Massachusetts. In the second place the Warrant granted in 1784 to the negroes gave them no authority to establish a Grand Lodge or a National Grand Lodge, it being nothing more than an ordinary Lodge Warrant. Thirdly, the Warrant from want of compliance with its provisions, even if it had been legally granted, became forfeited from its failures to make annual returns, and has long since been expunged from the roll of English Lodges.

Their recognition, therefore, would be an outrage on Masonic law and usage, and if they are visited here by persons claiming to be Masons, it is at the expense of their most solemn covenants.

(Walkes' Comments)

See "Niggerdom in Regalia" in Black Square and Compass, for it smacks of coming from the hand of Fitz Gerald Tisdall.

VOLUME XXII (August 1, 1863, Page 310)

(Williamson's Comments)

Under "Colored Lodge" there is the usual inaccurate matter about our Craft as expressed by a Representative of the Grand Lodge of Pennsylvania.

(From the Publication)

COLORED LODGES

After a careful examination of so much of the proceeding of our Right Worshipful Sister Grand Lodges on the subject of "Colored Lodges," and the action of some of the Right Worshipful Grand Lodges of Europe in regard to it, there is a fear on our mind, that the Masonic opinion held by the Grand Lodges of the United States thereto, may not have been strongly and clearly laid before those jurisdictions. The argument on this question is plain and conclusive. Each Grand Lodge in the United States is a sovereign and supreme jurisdiction. No subordinated Lodge of Freemasons can regularly exist in any jurisdiction, without its rights, privileges and powers being directly derived from such supreme sovereign authority. If any such Lodge claims to exist and work, it is not recognized as a Lodge of Freemasons — hence it is irregular or clandestine. No other Masonic authority than that of the jurisdiction can grant a right for such a Lodge.

No Grand Lodge in the United States has ever granted a Charter to a "Colored Lodge" of Freemasons. Then Colored Lodges are not recognized, and are either irregular or clandestine. As these "Colored Lodges" claiming to exist in the United States are not recognized by any Grand Lodge of the United States, they cannot be Masonically recognized anywhere. The principle is too plain to admit of controversy. If the Grand Lodges of the United States are supreme in their several jurisdictions, they are surely the highest Masonic authority known to such jurisdiction. If they are the highest and best authority, there is not a forum, which can claim an appellate power to review or overrule their decision. Their decision on any question which they have the sole right and power to decide, is absolute and steadfast. Then, if each Grand Lodge in the United States decides that "Colored Lodges" are not recognized as Masonic institutions within their jurisdiction, it is neither competent nor Masonic for any foreign Grand Lodge to set aside such decision. To do so would disturb the harmony, destroy the sovereignty, impair the dignity, usurp the rights and powers, and subordinate a Right Worshipful Grand Lodge. It would do more. It would cause its constituents to depend on any other authority but its own. The proposition thus stated is unanswerable. Thus the question stands, in the opinion of the Right Worthy Grand Lodge of Pennsylvania. It cannot be made to yield to any other than indisputable Masonic principles. No other elements must be permitted to enter into the discussions. Masonry knows Masonic principles, landmarks, rights, privileges and objects only. What is not of Freemasonry, is not within the power of Masonic action. Other questions may knock at the West door, but they ought not, cannot, will never be, allowed to enter into a Temple dedicated to Freemasonry – never, – Rep. G.L. Pen.

(Walkes' Comment)

We saw how sovereign the Caucasian Grand Lodges were 35 years later, when the Caucasian Grand Lodge of Washington recognized Prince Hall Freemasonry. When the sixteen Caucasian Grand Lodges declared "non-intercourse" giving lie to the concept that the writer has given, that each Grand Lodge is supreme in their several jurisdiction. While Caucasian Freemasonry may have never had a National Grand Lodge within their Masonic history, they employed National Grand Lodge powers. But Prince Hall Freemasonry has learned that our Caucasian counterparts talk from both sides of their mouths.

VOLUME XXV (May 1, 1866, Page 193)

(Williamson's Comments)

Under "Negro Lodges" we come to a very amusing story which runs as follows: Paul Drayton, during that period, was Grand Master of the Grand Lodge of New York (National Union), and in complexion he could be readily mistaken for a white man. He visited the State of North Carolina and began to establish Lodges among the colored people in his capacity of Grand Master of New York.

Without making any attempt to ascertain whether or not the Grand Master of New York (White) was invading the Tar Heel jurisdiction, some of the latter immediately began accusing the leader of the Craft in the Empire State with degrading Freemasonry through the initiation of black men, thereby, causing much ill feeling towards the northern grand body without the least justification. In due time, the North Carolina brethren learned to their chagrin they had made fools of themselves but the joke could not be easily forgotten.

A little over seven pages are devoted to the North Carolina and other incidents connected with the subject.

(From the Publication)

NEGRO LODGES

We have been favored with a copy of a remarkable report, adopted by the Grand Lodge of North Carolina in December last, on the existence of "Negro Lodges" in that State. The report sets forth that the "Past Most Worshipful Paul Drayton of the National Grand Lodge," has recently established in the city of Newbern, a Body, which he designates as "King Solomon's Lodge No. 1, A.F.M., composed entirely and exclusively of negroes," and that this was done "under the authority of the Most Worshipful Grand Lodge of the State of New York." On these alleged facts, the report proceeds to arraign the Grand Lodge of North Carolina. If these statements were true, and susceptible of the interpretation given to them in the report, they would constitute just cause of complaint on the part of our brethren of North Carolina; but if the subject had not imparted its own color to the perceptive difficulties of the committee, it would have occurred to them that there is not and never has been any body or organization in the United States which the Masonic fraternity do or ever have recognized as "A National Grand Lodge," and that Mr. Paul Drayton must have been a "Past Most Worshipful" of something unknown to the Masonry of this country, or that he was an impostor. This plain and obvious deduction from the facts would have saved the committee the labor of writing one of the most objectionable reports that ever emanated from an intelligent Grand Lodge — the direct tendency of which is to create jealousies and prejudices, not calculated to restore the community of fellowship and reciprocal confidence between the brethren of the North and the South, which the unhappy events of the last four years have done so much to disturb.

The committee says, "If the facts are true, the Grand Lodge of New York has sent an agent into the southern states with Full power to organize Lodges throughout the southern portion of the country,"and express the "opinion" that the Grand Lodge has "no such right." If there be anything fixed and certain in the Masonic law of this country, it is that no such right exists. The committee, however, "anxious to find something which would relieve their brethren of New York from what seems to be a breach of that courtesy, which so much distinguishes Masonic intercourse, have hope that it may turn out to be true, that there are still remaining in different portions of the South, New York troops, and that the purpose is simply to organize military Lodges among such troops." If such be the purpose, the committee concedes its propriety; but they ought to have been better informed than to suppose that Army Lodges were established by traveling missionaries. The usages of Masonry recognize no such practice. They, however, "are constrained to say, with much concern, that the impression made upon them by a careful consideration of the aforesaid articles is, that the purpose is not to organize Military Lodges, but to organize Lodges throughout the southern portion of the country generally, and especially

"Negro Lodges." This is the precise impression, whether so designed by the committee or not, that the report is calculated to make upon the entire southern mind; and a more mischievous and dangerous sentiment the ingenuity of the committee could not have originated. If it were possible for such a belief to find its way into the hearts of our southern brethren, it would work an entire and bitter separation of all Masonic intercourse and sympathy in the fraternity of the two sections of the country; and this with entire justice. It would be such a gross and palpable violation of the lawful rights and prerogatives of the Grand Lodges of the Southern States, that they could not submit to it for a moment, without compromising their own dignity and surrendering their existence as independent organizations. But it is charitable to believe that the committee did not comprehend the full force and effect of their own language.

The following paragraphs from the Report are scarcely less remarkable as coming from a southern source:

> "The committee do not, in the abstract, question the propriety of making Masons of negroes. Our ancient landmarks are that he that be made a Mason must be able in all degrees; that is, free born, worthy, and well qualified. It is not necessary that the candidate should be a white man. We teach that in every clime, and among every people, Masonry has existed; and to every human being our benevolence extends. But propriety, conformity to government, and reasonably, to religion, and to manners and customs, have distinguished our Order. Our communications are often breast to breast, mouth to ear. Fellowship, in the sense of the most perfect equality, intimate relationship, and close communication, is the chief characteristic of our intercourse."

We are not disposed to criticize this paragraph with much nicety, but that the committee does not "question the propriety of making Masons of negroes," comes with singular significance from a section of the country that, for more than half a century, has been consistent in its denunciations of the recognition, by Northern Grand Lodges, of colored men, who had been made Masons even in foreign countries and by lawful authority. Tempord mulantur, et nos mutaumur il illis.

If it be true that the Almighty never made a slave, and that slavery is a condition into which the child enters after birth, then it follows that his restoration to freedom restores him to all his natural right. The earliest regulation (1723) we have upon the subject declares that a candidate for Masonry must be "free born." This was soon afterwards (1738) explained by the addition of the words, "or no bondman." The Grand Lodge of England, adopting this interpretation, provides, by constitutional law, that the candidate must be a "freeman." The rule in this country is, that the mother must have been free at the time of the birth. This would of course exclude all the negroes of the South who were born into slavery; and this fact should quiet the nerves of our brethren of the North Carolina committee against having their sensibilities disturbed by being required to take their former slaves into their embraces as brethren, should there ever arise such a preposterous movement as that they so credulously attribute to the Grand Lodge of New York. They have manifestly been cheated out of their senses into a ridiculous absurdity. But let us follow them a step further:

> "We know that Masonry is not only close in fellowship, but it is perfect in morals, and intricate in science. And we know that the negroes of the South are wholly incompetent to embrace it. They are ignorant, uneducated, immoral, untruthful, and intellectually, they are more impotent than minority or dotage: both of which we exclude. It would be rare if any locality could furnish the requisite number of sufficient capacity to open a Lodge. Therefore to have Lodges exclusively of negroes would be dangerous to the high character of our Order. And to associate them in Lodges with our white brethren would be impossible."

If this be a true description of the character and condition of the blacks of the South, if they are "ignorant, uneducated, immoral, untruthful," and so much more intellectually debased than other classes, even in their "minority and dotage": it is not impertinent to inquire how they became so? And we will leave the committee to answer this question themselves:

> "We fear that our northern brethren are in gross error as to their Masonic mission to the South. Why should the mission be to the South? Why not to the negroes of the North? We fear that they are unconsciously imbued with the spirit of fanaticism; that they have unwholesome dreams that they are better than we. And we do allow ourselves to resist the conviction that we are not more devoted to the best interest of the negroes of the South than they can possibly be. They were born in our families; we have nursed them in sickness; labored with them in the field and in the shop. We have rejoiced with them when we had much, and suffered with them when we had little; we have protected them because they were weak, and advised them because they were ignorant. We have made them better than Africans, and nearly equal to our Northern brethren — themselves being judges, and, but for fanaticism, doubtless many of them would have been worthy of Masonic privileges. Our earnest desire now is, still further to improve their condition. We would educate them, improve their habits and manners, and make them industrious and provident."

If, under such a training, they have attained only to the stature of "ignorant, lying, immoral dotards," it might be question whether their longer continuance in the same school, and under the same teachers, would materially "improve their condition, their habits or their manners" in the future.

As to the "Masonic mission" mentioned by the committee, it is enough to say, that the only mission which the Masons of the North have to make to their brethren of the South is one of peace, brotherly love, and relief. We give them our sympathy, and contribute liberally of our substance; and what we ask in return is, that they treat us as brethren and not attribute to us acts and designs of which we are not guilty.

Here we leave this unfortunate report, in the hope and expectation that the Grand Lodge of North Carolina will avail itself of the earliest opportunity that may offer to repair the injustice it has done, not only to its sister Grand Lodge of New York, but to their brethren, generally, of the Northern States; and that they may the more clearly see the propriety of doing so, and the necessity of correcting the unauthorized statements and unfraternal structures of their committee, we will briefly sketch, for their information, the origin, and so far as we are able, the present status of African or "Negro Lodges" in this country.

In the early part of the year 1784, certain colored persons residing in Boston, and claiming to be Masons, petitioned the Honorable Thomas Howard, Earl of Effingham, acting Grand Master under His Royal Highness the Duke of Cumberland, Grand Master of the Grand Lodge of England, for a Charter, authorizing them to open and hold a Lodge of Freemasons in the town of Boston in the State of Massachusetts. This petition was entrusted to a Captain Scott, of the "London Packet," and by him taken out to London and placed in the hands of the proper Masonic authorities there. After some considerable delay, the reason for which is not known, the Charter prayed for was granted to Prince Hall, Boston Smith, Thomas Sanderson, and several others, all colored men, and inhabitants of Boston. It bears date September 29, 1784, and is signed by Rowland Holt, D.G. Master, and countersigned by William White, Grand Secretary. We think it probable that it also bears the name of the Duke of Cumberland, though of this we have no certain knowledge. We are also under the impression that the Charter was not received, nor the Lodge organized, until the year 1787. It was an ordinary Charter, drawn up in the usual form, and conferred no other privileges than those which are ordinarily granted by such instruments. Prince Hall was its first Master. He was an intelligent and influential man among persons of his own color. Of the other petitioners we have no knowledge; nor does it appear from anything that we have ever met with on the subject, where they obtained their Masonry, if they had any, or by what means they were enabled to satisfy the authorities at London that they were Masons. (It is said they were made in Army Lodges, but there is probably no authority for this). Scott, who was probably a member of the Order, may have aided them in this respect, as he did in obtaining their Charter. The Lodge continued in active operation for some years, when it fell into abeyance. Of its proceedings, from this time until 1827, we have no definite information. In the last-named year, we find it in active operation under the mastership of Mr. John T. Hilton, who, we believe claimed for it the powers and prerogative of a Grand Lodge; which powers it must, however, have assumed as early as 1812, in which year it is said to have granted a Charter for "Boyer Lodge, No. 1 (colored), of the City of New York." It was stricken from the registry of the Grand Lodge of England about the year 1813; and its lawful existence was then, of course, terminated, supposing it to have ever been anything other than an irregular organization, but it was never any thing else. Its original establishment in Boston was a violation of the jurisdictional rights of the Grand Lodges of Massachusetts; and, therefore, waiving the question of color, it could never have been recognized, by them or any other Masonic body, as a lawful Lodge. It never was so recognized; nor has there ever been, during the whole period of its existence, any recognition of its acts, or intercourse had with its members, by any Grand Lodge, or other Masonic body in this country.

Such is very briefly the origin of Lodges of colored Masons in America. Frequent attempts have been made to induce the Grand Lodge of Massachusetts to acknowledge the Lodge in this city, on the ground that it emanated from legal authority; but they have always been resisted, and all intercourse with it prohibited; not solely, and perhaps not principally, because it was composed of colored men, but, primarily, because it was instituted in violation of the law of Masonic jurisdiction; and secondly, because its Charter was, more than half a century ago, revoked and annulled by the Grand Lodge from which it emanated.

But there is one view of this subject which it may be useful to consider before it is too much embarrassed by prejudice or unavailing vituperation.

"Negro Lodges" exist among us to a much greater extent than is generally supposed. Our information on this point is to the following effect:

1. That there is a National Grand Lodge, with its Grand Master and Grand Secretary, at Philadelphia, having under its jurisdiction Grand Lodges (with subordinates) in the States of Massachusetts, Rhode Island, New York, New Jersey, Pennsylvania, Delaware, Maryland, District of Columbia, Ohio, Michigan, Indiana, Louisiana, and California.

2. That there are subordinate Lodges in most or all of the Western and Eastern States, not named above, except Maine, New Hampshire, and Vermont, and in the following additional Southern States, to wit: Virginia, North Carolina, South Carolina, Georgia and Kentucky, where Grand Lodges have not yet been organized.

3. That there is a Grand Chapter, Grand Encampment, Grand Consistory, 32°, and Supreme Council, 33°, all located at Philadelphia, the two former having subordinate bodies in several of the States. We understand further that the Consistory and Supreme Council claim to have derived their authority from the Grand Orient of Hayti, with which body the Grand Lodges above referred to are said to be in regular communication.

But of this we have seen no evidence. We have also heard a singular story of two of the continental Grand Lodges in connection with these parties; but our authority is not sufficiently definite or reliable. We give this information for the special benefit of our brethren of the North Carolina committee, to whom it will probably be new, and perhaps useful in quieting their nerves. They claim to be Masonic associations; but of this we have no means of judging. If they are so, they are clandestine and irregular, and with them the Masons of this country, whether North or South, can hold no intercourse or communication. But it does not follow from this that it is either wise, or prudent, or just, that we should denounce, proscribe, or revile them. We may regret their existence, or that they had not organized under some other name; but as they have not seen fit to do so, we cannot help ourselves, and must accept the fact as it is. From what we have been able to learn from their printed documents, from their periodicals, the by-laws of their Lodges, and the published addresses of their more intelligent members, we are led to believe that they are a moral and benevolent association, and that they are doing much to relieve the necessities, to improve the social condition, and elevate the intellectual status of their own people. If this be so, the purpose of their association is a commendable one, and they will receive, at least from that part of the community who care little for Masonic relations, the encouragement which in their changed condition they so much need, and which is so essential to their personal welfare and usefulness. And, as from the peculiar nature of the case, whatever may be the character of their organizations, whether quasi-Masonic or otherwise, they can neither interfere with or impose upon our Lodges, or in any other way become troublesome to us, we, as Masons, need not be very sensitive on account of their existence among us. They will take care of themselves; and our true policy is to allow them to do so without interference from us. Supposing them to be irregular Masons, there is a wide distinction between their Lodges and similar clandestine bodies which are from time–to–time springing into existence under the patronage of men less honest in their purposes, though of whiter skins. In the latter case a fraud is practiced upon the credulous, and, if opportunity offers, an imposition upon the lawful Lodges of the country. In the former case, no such fraud is chargeable. They hold out no encouragement to their people that they will ever be recognized as Masons anywhere beyond their own circle; and it would be a mark of greater stupidity than their worst enemies give them credit for, if they should ever attempt to pass themselves off as Masons among those of a different class, in this country at least. Whatever might be the effect should any of them emigrate to Hayti, or other of the West India Islands, or England, or wherever else the color of the skin is not a disqualification for admission to a Masonic

Lodge, supposing them to know enough of Masonry to pass the required examination, it is impossible to say; nor is it a matter about which we need concern ourselves. There are safeguards enough for their protection; and if our brethren, in jurisdictions beyond the United States, fail to avail themselves of them, they alone are responsible for the consequences. We trust, therefore, in view of the whole matter, that our Grand Lodges, both North and South, will allow the subject to subside. No good can result from the further agitation of it, at least not until it shall assume a more serious aspect, than it at present wears.

(Walkes' Comments)

Paul Drayton was the first Grand Master of the Prince Hall Grand Lodge of New York. A drawing of him appears on page 125 of William H. Grimshaw's so-called, "Official History of Freemasonry." Harry E. Davis notes in his "History" that Drayton was made in a white Lodge in Charleston, South Carolina. His father, a white man, was a prominent citizen of that place, having served as a member of Congress, and his mother was a mulatto. As he was fair in complexion, it is probable that his colored lineage was not known at the time, as he was educated in the white schools. The incident is also mentioned on page 50 in Harold Van Buren Voorhis' "Negro Masonry in the United States." I agree with Bro. Williamson, the whole incident is quite amusing.

Because of space restraint, I will not be able to continue this paper. It would seem that I have used much more pages than I had expected when I first sat down and began to transcribe the material from the Williamson paper and the Freemasons' Monthly Magazine. I, however, will hope to continue this in a later paper.

ADDENDUM

On page 12 of this paper, there is mentioned the petition of the President of the Republic of Liberia to the Caucasian Grand Lodge of the District of Columbia. While the petition was voted out of hand, without so much as a discussion, I thought that I would investigate it further and in the proceedings of this same Grand Lodge dated December 27, A.L. 5852 under the Committee of Correspondence is found:

> Connecticut – "Reference is made to the action of our Grand Lodge on the petition for a Charter in the Republic of Liberia, and they say:
>
> We are willing to make due allowance for the very natural prejudices of our Southern brethren. We should even doubt the propriety of initiating colored men into the mysteries of Masonry in any of the Lodges in the United States, or of instituting new Lodges here for their benefit. But as the Republic of Liberia is assuming an elevated position among the nations of the earth; as she is inhabited by a race of free and intelligent men and is unquestionably destined to exert a great and solitary influence in the civilization and Christianization of the whole vast continent of Africa, we can see no good reason for denying to the benign principles of Free Masonry the high privilege of contributing their proper share to the consummation of this great and glorious work. As at present advised, were the same petitioners whose prayer was rejected by our enlightened brethren of the Federal District, now to ask from this Grand Lodge a Charter for a Lodge to be established at Monrovia, we should feel it our duty to favor the granting of the prayer of the petition.
>
> We are willing to make all due allowance for the very natural philanthropic feelings of our Northern Brother, who penned this bid, for the honor of introducing Masonry among a nation of men, very few of whom can possess one of the essential requisites of a "good man and true," but we would most earnestly claim for our Grand Lodge, from our sister Grand Lodges, the merit of acting in the sphere of our duty from higher motives than natural prejudice against the colored man, and if not from any other consideration, demand, as coming within the scope of brotherly courtesy, some consideration for that action before its effect should be nullified by another Grand Body who ought to be governed by like action, upon like points of fact. Your Committee would simply ask, if a colored man, now free, but who was born a slave, should demand admission at the door of Subordinate Lodge of Connecticut, and that Lodge was unrestricted, entirely, as to the mere question of color, whether, that Grand Lodge would sanction the admission of such person?

President Joseph Jenkins Roberts, the "Father of Liberia" was never a slave. See the Second Quarter, 1981 issue of The Phylaxis magazine, beginning page 38.

COMMENTS FROM ROBERT L. DARBY, F.P.S. (Life)

Our illustrious brother has written a very lengthy piece that can only be characterized as both good and bad. Good in the sense that it sheds some light on the fraternal atmosphere of the nineteenth century; bad in the sense that today we are in no better shape than our brethren 142 years ago.

I especially enjoyed the remarks made by John T. Hilton in the last paragraph when he states, "that they were entirely independent of all white lodges, asked no favors of them, and would have nothing to do with them."

I consider it to be an error in judgment on the part of Mr. Hilton not to show the Charter to the R.W. Charles W. Moore, Grand Secretary of the Grand Lodge of Massachusetts. Allowing the gentleman to view the Charter could have made all the difference in the world in our status.

I love the way the Caucasian mind operates. How can a Charter for a Masonic Lodge named and styled "African" be obtained surreptitiously?

Trying to keep up with who is making comments at any given time, tends to make this paper difficult to read.

COMMENTS FROM ROBERT L. CANNADY, M.P.S.

In my opinion, I feel Bro. Walkes has written a masterpiece of literature in "Williamson's Out of the Past," but at the same time I feel with all the valuable information it contains, it is rather complicated for some of the members of the craft.

I am not saying by any means that my brothers are ignorant, but we are trying to reach the grass root brethren as well as the highly educated brethren, therefore I feel this beautiful paper should be made more simplified for that purpose alone. Remember, we have our brethren from all walks of life.

I must say Bro. Walkes has done a magnificent piece of research and certainly deserves to be complimented. I shall go so far as to quote our Ill. G.M. H.A. "This is a beautiful piece of work and the composer who wrote it is worthy of the confidence of the craft, and in due time shall receive his reward."

Brother Walkes has divulged a world of information pertaining to Prince Hall Masons, which should be read by all Masons, white as well as black. This will let these masons know where we Prince Hall Masons have come from, all of the obstacles which we had to hurdle in the past and are still confronting by certain narrow-minded people.

Bro. Walkes also mentions the purchase of a slave by one of the Demolays in Richmond, VA. I concur with the Good Bro. Walkes on this situation because there were Caucasian Lodges and Chapters that were left slaves by a passing Brother or Companion. Besides, the so-called Father of America owning slaves, Thomas Jefferson, our third president, and also a member of the Craft owned many slaves, and was also the Father of some of his slaves.

Also, one of the things that irked me while reading of the committee of the G.L. of N.C. is when they mentioned Prince Hall as being an intelligent man among persons of his own color. ***Why not among mankind instead?*** As Bro. Walkes often stated, and I agree with him, "There are two Americas, one black and one white." The sooner we get rid of that stigma, the better for America. As the late Langston Hughes would say, "Let America be America again."

Bro. Walkes, you have done a tremendous piece of writing and I congratulate you on it. Just simplify it for the Grass Root Brethren.

As proof of what Bro. Walkes is saying in this astonishing paper, all brothers should read, "Freemasonry Among Negroes and Whites in America," by Bro. Harvey Newton Brown.

Bro. Walkes, I take my hat off to you, just keep up the good work.

The Origin and Concept of Freemasonry: Another Look

by Tommy Rigmaiden, FPS
(1997 Edition)

The legends of Freemasonry are factual, as told in the historical events of the Volume of Sacred Law. These legends are indeed a living story. As tenets and teachings, such were applicable to the early craft of Freemasonry and equally applicable to the brethren of today, as they will be of those tomorrow. In this sense, Freemasonry, eliminates the term "myth."

If we were to look upon Freemasonry, as an invention or creation, where would we truly begin to look? One would think that, in doing so, we would have to go back to the oldest known origin, sign, legend, or initiation rite to begin our research. Any documentation of evidence that is consistent or compatible with the tradition of Freemasonry, must be honestly challenged. For example, Mattel started out with a creation or invention of the toy M-15 assault rifle. From this came a prototype assault rifle for the U.S. Military, with all of its revision, until this very day. Most of the time, if we carefully examined the past, we could get a very good picture of the place where things originated.

A performing artist who records a song about the Crucifixion at Calvary can not make such a song if he is not familiar with the events that took place some two thousand years ago. An artist cannot sensibly paint a portrait of Moses and the Exodus unless he has some insight into such an event. It is likewise with Freemasonry. This superstructure of the ancient craft cannot exist without a basic foundation. That foundation has to correlate consistently with the oldest known documents, whether they are ancient legends, historical accounts, or recorded events.

What finer example is there to which one may look for the origin and precepts of Freemasonry than what God the Almighty has shown us. For He took the finest of Operative Masons, whom He endowed with skills and within whose bosom He placed craftsmanship. As a result, a temple was laid and rebuilt under the divine order of the

Supreme Architect of the Universe.

As a further loving and divine extension, God sent His only begotten Son to greet and meet the brethren here on earth. Jesus Christ became that incorruptible temple, a temple raised from a dead level to a living perpendicular within that mystical number of days, three. One comes to quickly learn that Christ became that true stone that the builders rejected. To truly understand the origin and concept of Freemasonry, we must come to a realization that the Grand Ruler has circumscribed all things within due bounds. Jesus Christ, as a continued message, has laid the true foundation for all things by His words, His actions, and His everlasting Gospel of Brotherly Love. To fully understand Freemasonry, one must observe that Masonry's ideals and moral precepts transcend "Eurocentric definition." One need only to look at the life of Christ to understand that His Gospel is directed to the entire best interest of a family of common humanity, the high and the low, the rich and the poor. We can look at the lives of the early Christians and see that they shared all things in common. This is stated throughout the New Testament, which pictures a first-century church in which none went without their needs being met, and all shared in meeting the moral, spiritual, and physical needs of one another.

You see here the precepts of a commonality that expands through the Old and New Testaments. There is a phrase used during the installation ceremony of a High Priest which states: "As it was in the beginning, is now, and shall forever be, world without end." If, in the beginning, God said: "You are made in my likeness and image," and if from this one, "Adam," came this great nation of people, are we not one under the Fatherhood of Him who created us?

I would like to focus now on an article by Brother Michael L. Brodsky, entitled, "Some Reflections on the Origins of the Royal Arch," which was published in **Ars Quatuor Coronatorum: Transactions of Quatuor Coronati Lodge No. 2076, vol. 102 (1989)** In Brother Brodsky's "Introduction," he began by stating:

> In any attempt to uncover the early years of the Royal Arch or, for that matter, of Freemasonry in general, the Masonic historian has few reliable, authentic and useful documents with which to work. To understand the evolution of the craft, from the first authentic remaining material, using indirect evidence until history can be documented with written letters, minutes, etc., it is necessary to examine critically all the facts in our possession. Using all of the available evidence whatever its origin, provided its authenticity can be demonstrated, it is possible for the historian to build hypotheses which may later be proved correct or faulty as new, authentic, and relevant facts come to light. This is an accepted scientific procedure and, within the last few years, even some theories promoted by highly qualified historians have fallen victim to new analysis and the more careful interpretations of known or more recently discovered documents...

> The Royal Arch manuscript rituals in our possession today were written after 1780, but the content of the legend, or some of its fragments, as narrated now, was already known and used many years before that date in other Masonic rituals, though not necessarily ones commonly used or known in England.

I could not agree more with the last statement. There is more than one pocket on a shirt. There is the pocket on the left and the one on the right. You see, sometimes we look only in the left pocket on a shirt for knowledge concerning Freemasonry. But, I tell you, we must come to understand that there is another pocket, one that has been there all the time. We shall look into this other pocket shortly.

Now I shall turn to another author, one that I feel contributed greatly to the understanding of the Order of Knights Templar: the late John J. Robinson. In Brother Robinson's first book, *Born in Blood: The Lost Secrets of Freemasonry*, there are several interesting remarks, but, at this point, I shall only examine the following:

> Another important feature of today's initiation, which may have been absent in ancient rituals, is the Bible or other Holy Books on the Altar, used always in combination with the symbolic compass and square in the administration of the controversial oaths. It is hardly likely that a Bible was readily available to every little group throughout Britain in the fourteenth and fifteenth centuries, so the oath may well have been administered with a symbol only.

Here I must stop and ask the following question: "Has the author truly understood the oaths of Freemasonry, and the penalties of the same?" Let us visit the Holy Bible for a brief moment and see what is said of the Masonic oaths. We shall use as a reference the Masonic edition of the "King James Version," as published by A. J. Holman in 1968. Under the questions and answers pertaining to the symbolism of Masonry and its connection with the Bible, the editor asked:

> "How were the old Jewish Covenants performed?"

And answered:

> "The first mention of a covenant in the form that is met within the scripture is that recorded in the fifteenth chapter of Genesis, where, to confirm it, Abraham in obedience to Divine command, took a heifer, a she-goat, and a ram, and divided them in the midst, and laid each piece one against the other."

In the book of Jeremiah, there is another allusion to these ceremonies and the dangers of violation of the covenant are also expressed. Such ceremonies were performed in full as described. The parties entering into a covenant first selected a proper animal, such as a calf or a kid among the Jews, a sheep among the Greeks, or a pig among the Romans. The throat was then cut across with a single blow, so as to completely divide the windpipe and arteries without touching the bone. This was the first ceremony of the covenant. The second was to tear open the breast, to take from thence the heart and vitals. If, on inspection, the least imperfection was discovered, the body was considered unclean and thrown aside for another. The third ceremony was to divide the body in twain, and to place the two parts to the north and south, so that the parties to the covenant might pass between them coming from the east and going to the west. The carcass was then left as prey to the wild beasts of the field and the vultures of the air, and, thus, the covenant ratified. Most Masonic students can readily understand how these old Hebrew covenants parallel Speculative Science as a part of the basis of the system. See ***Jeremiah 34: 18-20***.

A covenant is an ancient ceremony. Not only were there sacrifices but there was also a memorial made during this occasion. Some kind of pillar, column, or building would be set up to remind the people of their covenant. It might have the conditions of the covenant chiseled upon them. The Temple could have been used as a reminder of the covenant between two parties, as during the time of King Solomon's Temple. In the book of Amos, as translated in the New American Version of the Bible, chapter 1 verse 9 states:

> Thus says the Lord: for three crimes of Tyre, and for four, I will not revoke my word; Because they delivered whole groups captive to Edom, and did not remember the pact of brotherhood.

You see, Hiram of Tyre made a pact (covenant, if you will) with Solomon and called him "brother."

The following question comes to mind: "Can the covenant be broken?" Some of the conditions were certainly not kept during the time of the Israelites. Some of the old prophets felt that the covenant could not be broken because God was the main party to the covenant. Thus, they reasoned, God is always faithful; it was Israel that was not always faithful. So it is always a point made to call people back to faithfulness, repentance, and to living up to the conditions of the covenant, to being God's people. The results of such a call should be positive rather than negative. Some say that the covenant is never broken, but that most do not fulfill their obligations. Now, we have come to learn that we do not see a sacrificial covenant any more, because Christ made the supreme sacrifice. However, we should also remember that He left us with something of much more intrinsic value. It is called the Holy Communion, or the Holy Eucharist. During this mystical occasion, as we come into communion, we come to understand that we are truly one in Christ Jesus. And, during that intimate "Fellowship," we can truly say:

> "We love you, Lord, and we love our brothers and sisters."

Now, if we look at the meaning of the word "brotherhood," according to Webster's Dictionary, 9th ed., the word means:

> "Fellowship, alliance, or a whole body of persons engaged in business or a profession."

If we look at the word "communion," it is defined as:

> "An intimate fellowship or rapport; and a body of Christians having a common faith and discipline."

Lastly, let us examine the word "community," which is defined as:

> "People with a common interest living in a particular area," or "Fellowship."

To ask of anyone to live in such a relationship, as has been examined, would in and of itself require one to act within a certain law, or policy, which would impose some amount of agreement, if you will. Thus, the New Covenant, as set down by Christ, asks that we live as true brothers and sisters, realizing that we are all members of one body. With this word of thought (as expressed by the Greek word Logos), how can Freemasonry, in all of its grandeur, not call a member's attention to the importance of keeping his covenant? Does not such a covenant exist within one's own heart?

Freemasonry, Another Look

To further expound on the issue of where and how the ideal of Freemasonry evolved, let us look at the Essenes, a first-century Jewish sect whose most famous community was Qumran, which was located by the Dead Sea. The Essenes have been described as a Jewish brotherhood. Although they are not mentioned by name in the New Testament, some scholars believe that both John the Baptist and Jesus may have spent time with them. The New Testament contains many references to love for one another, charity, alms-giving, sharing, obedience, and respect.

As one of our beloved Grand Masters of Prince Hall Masonry has plainly stated, and I can not agree with him more,

> "Freemasonry begins within the confines of one's heart, and it is called Love. As it was in the beginning, now and forever shall be, world without end, Amen, so mote it be."

If one truly wishes to understand Freemasonry, one cannot begin that understanding without going back to the source of that understanding, which was the Logos or "Word," the Word that was made flesh and dwelled among us. So the least ideal of a

Eurocentric definition of Freemasonry was an attempt to start the search for truth in the middle of the sixteenth and seventeenth century. But the ultimate quest for the origin of the Brotherhood of Man under the Fatherhood of God begins with His Word.

I am somewhat amazed at the subject presented in E. E. Oglivie's book entitled, *Freemasons' Royal Arch Guide*, where the author stated:

> How many original Grand Lodges do we commemorate? Three, Most Excellent. Name them. The first or holy lodge; the second or sacred lodge; and the third or grand and royal lodge. Where was the first or holy lodge holden? At the foot of Mount Horeb in the wilderness of Sinai. Who presided? Moses, Aholiab, and Bezaleel. Where was the second or sacred lodge holden? In the bosom of Mount Moriah. Who presided? Solomon, King of Israel, Hiram, King of Tyre; and Hiram Abiff. Where was the third, or grand and royal lodge holden? At Jerusalem. Who presided? Zerubbabel, Prince of the people; Haggai the Prophet; and Joshua, the son of Josedech the High Priest. Companions, let us attend to the pious memory of those Grand Originals.

If there ever was a concept—and I believe there was—an idea or a call to community, an idea of intimate fellowship, an idea of communion, it most certainly would have been the case, as mentioned in the statement above, on "How many original grand lodges do we commemorate?" You see, my brethren, the Lord always calls forth those whom He wishes, to get a promise fulfilled. And on each occasion, He always calls on those He needs in groups of three. There is a direct underlying meaning here: that mankind is a dependent being. To further confirm my understanding, if you will, let us look at an object that has come to be recognized as the "World's Oldest Poorbox."

The Bar Magazine

In *Biblical Archaeology Review*, 18 (November/December, 1992), there is an article by Gabriel Barkay, entitled, "The World's Oldest Poorbox." For eighty years, a bowl laid neglected in Jerusalem's Rockefeller Museum. The bowl has a typically Judean form, dateable to the late eighth century B.C. Only an enigmatic inscription, incised just below the rim on the inside, suggested that the bowl may be special. Barkay stated:

> I believe that this inscription was intended to signify that contributions to the poor were to be placed in the bowl. The bowl was probably placed in a cultic location, a temple, shrine, or high place. The inscription was an instruction to worshipers to deposit into the bowl commodities that, by Biblical law, they were required to give to their 'poor brothers.' The contents were then distributed by the Priests to the needy. In ancient Israelite society, there was a bond of brotherhood between all members, which was sometimes extended to include 'Mankind

as a whole.' Thus, the term 'brother' appears in many Biblical laws, especially those related to social justice.

Brother

This term was used in the ancient Near East to denote someone of equal rank or status. It also appears, in this sense, in an inscription on one of the famous Arad Ostraca and in international correspondences. In these sources, "brother" stands in contrast to "father" and "son," which indicate superior and inferior status respectively. In the Biblical laws referring to social justice, the poor are called "your brother" and even "your poor brother." For example, in Deuteronomy 15:11, we are commanded: "Open thy hand wide unto thy poor and needy brother." See also Leviticus 25:25, 35-40, 47-48; and Deuteronomy 15:7-8, 11-15.

The crops of the seventh year were to be set aside for the poor, according to Exodus 23:10-11 and Leviticus 25:4-6. Moreover, the tithe of the third year was not to be brought to the Temple but, instead, was intended for the poor and the less privileged sectors of Israelite society, and could be eaten locally, according to Deuteronomy 14:28-29 and 26:12-13. It is in this context that we must understand the inscription inside the *Beth Shemesh* bowl. Thus, the inscribed bowl was apparently meant to contain food for the poor, who were called, echoing the Bible, "your brother."

One cannot but find a direct relationship, in the article above. I cannot but feel that Freemasonry existed from the very beginning of time. True Masonry, I believe, is not necessarily contained within the Masonic ritual, but is found in the man with a heart of love, implanted with the Holy Spirit by God. In a charge, delivered to the brethren of African Lodge No. 459, on the 25th of June 1792, Right Worshipful Master Prince Hall, one of our forefathers, gave us another pocket from which to choose. In his book *Prince Hall: Life and Legacy*, Dr. Charles H. Wesley quoted the following words of Prince Hall:

> The next thing is love and benevolence to all the family of mankind, as God's make and creation, therefore we ought to love them all, for love or hatred is of the whole kind, for if I love a man for the sake of the image of God, which is on him, I must love all, for he made all, and upholds all, and we are dependent upon him for all we do enjoy, and expect to enjoy, in this world and that which is to come.—Therefore he will help and assist all his fellow-men in distress, let them be of what colour or nation they may, yea, even our very enemies, much more a brother Mason. I shall therefore give you a few instances of this from Holy Writ, and first, how did Abraham prevent the storm, or rebellion that was rising between Lot's servants and his? Saith Abraham to Lot, 'let thee be no strife I pray thee between me and thee, for the land is before us, if you will go to the left, then I will go to the right, and if you will go to the right, then I will go to the

left.' They divided, and peace was restored. I will mention the compassion of a blackman (sic) to a Prophet of the Lord. Ebedmelech, when he heard that Jeremiah was cast into the dungeon, he made intercession for him to the King, and got liberty to take him out from the jaws of death. See Jer. xxxvii, 7-13...

I shall just mention the good deeds of the Samaritan, though at that time they were looked upon as unworthy to eat, drink or trade with their fellow-men, at least by the Jews; see the pity and compassion he had on a poor distrest and half dead stranger. See Luke x. from 30 to 37. See that you endeavour to do so likewise.—But when we consider the amazing condescending love and pity our blessed Lord had on such poor worms as we are, as not only to call us his friends, but his brothers, we are lost and can go no further in holy writ for examples to excite us to the love of our fellow-men—But I am aware of an objection that may arise (for some men will catch at any thing) that is that they were not all masons; we allow it, and I say that they were not all Christians, and their benevolence to strangers ought to shame us both, that there is so little, so very little of it to be seen in these enlightened days.

The Samaritans may well have understood the precepts of brotherly support and assistance to a poor and distressed human being. I find it quite interesting that, in a work published by Time-Life Books, entitled, T*ime Frame, 3000-1500 B.C.: The Age of the God-Kings*, there is a Samaritan ceremonial vessel, pictured with several details upon it. But the most impressive thing about this vessel—and what caught my immediate attention—were the characters at the very top of the ceremonial vessel. This ancient piece of precious art work has on it, what appears to be, a square and compass, with a straight line in the center. It appears several times at the very top of the vessel. The other thing that strikes me oddly, is that this vessel is dated around 3000 B.C. This would predate King Solomon's and even King David's time. So, if we try to link the emblematic shield of David or Solomon to that of our present-day Masonic emblem, then should we not take the Samaritans' ceremonial vessel into account? Would it not be the oldest or among the oldest known marks, characters, or emblems of mankind? I have found no other emblem anywhere that has almost the exact features of the emblems of Freemasonry. This great piece of art work is located in the *Musee du Louvree/Reunion des Musees Nationaux,* in Paris.

Dr. Leonard Jeffries, Jr., a Black professor at New York City College, stated on the *African-American Journal* television series, during the "Fourth Annual World Melanin Conference," in Dallas, Texas, that many of the ancient philosophers were, in fact, educated at the ancient Luxor Temple in Egypt, and then returned to build the western empires. Dr. Jeffries further stated that this same Temple is the place where the ideals of the Masonic, Eastern Star, and Odd Fellows movements originated. In June 1991, I wrote to Dr. Jeffries on this subject but I did not receive a reply.

We shall now return to Prince Hall's charge to African Lodge No. 459. In this great message, this highly esteemed brother stated:

> I shall now shew you what progress Masonry hath made since the siege and taking of Jerusalem in the year 70, by Titus Vespacian; after a long and bloody siege, a million of souls having been slain or had perished in the city, it was taken by storm and the city set on fire. There was an order of men called the order of St. John, who besides their other engagements, subscribed to another, by which they bound themselves to keep up the war against the Turks. These men defended the temple when on fire, in order to save it, so long that Titus was amazed and went to see the reason of it; but when he came so near as to behold the *Sanctum Sanctorum*, he was amazed, and shed tears, and said no wonder these men should so long to save it. He honored them with many honors, and large contributions were made to that order from many kingdoms; and were also knighted. They continued 88 years in Jerusalem, till that city was again retaken by the Turks, after which they resided 104 years in the Cyrean city of Ptolemy, till the remains of the Holy Conquest were lost. Whereupon they settled on the Island of Cyprus, where they continued 18 years, till they found an opportunity to take the Island Rhodes; being masters of that, they maintained it for 213 years, and from thence they were called Knights of Rhodes, till in the year 1530 they took their residence in the Island of Malta, where they have continued to this day, and are distinguished by the name of the Knights of Malta. Their first Master was Villaret in the year 1099. Fulco Villaret in the year 1322, took the Island of Rhodes, and was after that distinguished by the title of Grand-Master, which hath devolved to his Successors to this day.

This speech, delivered during a time frame when most men were uneducated, is undoubtedly a very important impressive source of information. If we were to look at the forefathers of whom Prince Hall also spoke in his charge as examples to imitate, we can quickly learn that there is a direct religious tie. The great Tertullian spoke in great detail about the first-century initiation rites of baptism, and the procedures used therein. One could quickly identify with the ceremonies that occurred during that period. Saint Augustine is mentioned in Paul Johnson's book, *A History of Christianity,* as having been introduced and escorted about several countries by Freemasons. According to Johnson:

> Augustine himself went to Rome and later Milan, on the Manichee "net," a freemason, which provided him with contacts and jobs. It is not absolutely clear when he became a Christian convert.

Another article of interest is the "Knights of Malta," of which Prince Hall spoke in his charge. In *The Book of the Popes*, compiled by the Benedictine monks of the Saint Augustine Abby, called "Ramsgate," it is stated regarding the Knights of Malta:

> The Pontificate of Innocent VIII, witnessed a further decline in the prestige of the papacy. The Pope no longer considered it his duty to urge a crusade but, instead, entered into negotiations with the Sultan of the Turks, which centered on the person of the Turkish Prince Djem, secured by the Pope in March, 1489. The Prince, who claimed the throne occupied by his brother Bayazid II, had been detained by the Knights of Rhodes with whom he had taken refuge and was eventually handed over by them to the Pope, in return for the grant of a Cardinalate to their Grand Master. Pope Innocent treated him as a princely guest, even receiving him into the Consistory. The most striking evidence of the Pope's lack of interest in a crusade, is the fact that he received an annual subsidy from the Sultan in return for keeping Djem in captivity.

The foregoing article is simply awesome. But we must continue our search and understanding of Freemasonry by looking in the other pocket for available resources. There have been many well-written works on subjects related to Freemasonry. But, until we look at history in its totality, we are, in fact, simply withdrawing a cup of water from the bucket of knowledge on the subject of Freemasonry, its origins and concepts. As for me, this brief research paper is not intended as a total picture of the origin of Freemasonry. But it brings home the fact that much is left to be examined when it comes to the ancient craft. I am firmly convinced that Prince Hall Freemasonry is more than capable of contributing its share in the development of an overall picture and concept of Freemasonry as a whole. The search for Masonic truth, therefore, continues to move on, and it is up to every member of the craft, regardless of where they are dispersed, to share in this great and important undertaking.

COMMENTS ON "THE ORIGIN AND CONCEPT OF FREEMASONRY"

by Dr. Robert L. Uzzel, FPS

I wish to thank Brother Rigmaiden for a very interesting paper. I have long contended that, while the history of modern Speculative Masonry cannot be traced back further than the eighteenth century, the roots of Freemasonry are quite ancient and diverse.

The American Heritage Dictionary defines "freemasonry" (with lowercase "f") as, "Spontaneous fellowship and sympathy among a number of people," and "Freemasonry" (with the capital "F") as "The institutions, precepts, and rites of Freemasons." The former definition could apply to a wide variety of organizations. On the sinister side, I once read a description of the mob led by Al Capone in Chicago as a "freemasonry of crookdom."

The majority of Masonic historians trace the beginnings of Freemasonry to the Operative Masons who worked on the cathedrals during the Middle Ages. Over time, it is contended that Operative Masonry evolved into Speculative Masonry. However, in recent years, this view has been challenged by a number of writers, including Brother John J. Robinson, who is quoted by Brother Rigmaiden. Robinson, who held the firm conviction that the real roots of Freemasonry were found in the Knights Templar, rather than in Operative Masonry, contributed more to Freemasonry during the past four years of his life than most Masons contributed during a lifetime. His first book, *Born in Blood: The Lost Secrets of Freemasonry*, appeared in 1989. The sequel, *Dungeon, Fire and Sword: The Knights Templar in the Crusades*, was published two years later. He completed the manuscript for his last book, *A Pilgrim's Path: Freemasonry and the Religious Right*, in 1992. Ironically, he was not a Mason at the time. His value as a non-Masonic defender of the fraternity delayed his application for membership. He received his first degree in the Fall of 1992. Complications of cancer prevented his return to the lodge. Ohio Grand Master Ray Evans conferred the remaining degrees "at sight" in the hospital. Likewise, he received the 33rd degree from Scottish Rite Grand Commander Robert Ralston in the hospital on 3 September 1993—only three days before his death.

Brother Rigmaiden gave an interesting discussion of the concept of covenant. He wrote:

> "We do not see a sacrificial covenant any more, because Christ made the supreme sacrifice. However, we should also remember that He left us with something much more intrinsic in value. It is called the Holy Communion, or the Holy Eucharist. During this mystical occasion, as we come into communion, we come to understand that we are truly one in Christ Jesus."

I fully agree with this interpretation of this blessed sacrament. Brother Rigmaiden is both a Roman Catholic and a Freemason who "enjoys the best of both worlds." Although I am not a Catholic, I often go to mass, never missing on Christmas Eve. I have many Catholic friends, including a number of priests. I have taught many Catholic students. I have received Catholic communion many times and have even assisted a priest in serving it. I hope that, in the near future, I will have the experience of preaching in a Catholic Church. Like my favorite theologian, Dr. Harvey Cox of Harvard (whose boyhood home in Malvern, Pennsylvania was located between a Baptist Church and a Catholic Church), I feel close to Catholicism yet outside of it. As an ecumenist, I long for the day when all churches will have open communion, with believers of all denominations invited to the Lord's table. When love prevails, differences over the "Real Presence" may be viewed as matters of semantics. I also long for the day when clergy of all denominations can freely exchange pulpits without raising any eyebrows.

Brother Rigmaiden pointed out that such conflicts between Catholicism and Freemasonry are rooted in misunderstandings going back to the Crusades and that such should not be allowed to govern Catholic-Masonic relations today. More Catholic-Masonic dialogue is needed. Brother Rigmaiden and other Catholic Masons have much to contribute to this dialogue. I appreciate his letter to Bishop Fabian Bruskewitz of Lincoln, Nebraska in opposition to the excommunication of Masons in his diocese. By the way, a priest of the Carmelite Order recently informed me that the Bishop Bruskewitz is totally out of step with the vast majority of American Catholics.

Brother Rigmaiden wrote:

> "If one truly wishes to understand Freemasonry, one cannot begin that understanding without going back to the source of that understanding, which was the *Logos* or 'Word,' the Word that was made flesh and dwelled among us."

I fully agree with this statement. Regarding the *Logos* in Masonry, the following statement is found on page 251 of Albert Pike's *Morals and Dogma*:

> To Philo, the Supreme Being was the Primitive Light, or the Archetype of Light, Source whence the rays emanate that illuminate Souls. He was also the Soul of the Universe, and as such acted in all its parts. He Himself fills and limits His whole Being. His Powers and Virtues fill and penetrate all. These Powers (*dunameis*) are Spirits distinct from God, the "Ideas" of Plato personified. He is without beginning, and lives in the prototype of Time (*aion*).
>
> His image is THE WORD (Logos), a form more brilliant than fire; that not being the *pure* light. This LOGOS dwells in God, for the Supreme Being makes to Himself, within His Intelligence, the types or ideas of everything that is to become reality in this World. The LOGOS is the vehicle by which God acts on the Universe, and may be compared to the speech of man.

> The LOGOS being the World of Ideas (*kosmos noetos*), by means whereof God has created visible things, he is the most ancient God, in comparison with the World, which is the youngest production. THE LOGOS, *Chief of Intelligence*, of which He is the general representative, is named *Archangel*, *type*, and *representative* of all spirits, even those of mortals.

Toward the end of his paper, Brother Rigmaiden provided an interesting discussion of the Knights of Malta. On page 471 of *Dungeon, Fire, and Sword*, Robinson wrote regarding this fascinating order:

> The present ponderous designation of the Hospitallers reflects their long history of survival: The Sovereign Military Hospitaller Order of St. John of Jerusalem, of Rhodes, and of Malta. The Hospitallers completed their conquest of the island of Rhodes in 1310, while the Knights Templar still languished in prison. They continued to provide help in holding the Muslims in check, but more and more as a naval force, rather than as a land army of mounted knights. In 1522, the Hospitallers were driven off Rhodes by the Turks, prompting them to seek another sea base in order to maintain their position as a naval power. In 1530, their search was rewarded when the Emperor Charles V granted the island of Malta. From their new base, the Hospitallers acted as a buffer between Christian Europe and Muslim North Africa, earning the popular new name of the Knights of Malta. In 1798, the order lost Malta to Napoleon Bonaparte, who, in turn, lost it to the British. In 1834, the Knights of Malta established their present headquarters in Rome, where they are regarded by the Vatican as a sovereign power.

It is interesting to note that the word "hospital" was derived from this order, whose members cared for sick pilgrims en route to the Holy Land. It is also significant that there was a long history of conflict between the Hospitallers and the Templars, which at times included open warfare. When the latter were officially suppressed in England, all of their property was given to the former. The crux of Robinson's theory is that the British Templars continued to operate underground for four hundred years, at times committing acts of revenge against the Hospitallers and eventually surfacing as Freemasons. In view of the hostility between the two orders, it is indeed ironic that the two have been brought together in the Commandery degrees of the York Rite.

Brother Rigmaiden described much of Masonic research as "simply withdrawing a cup of water from the bucket of knowledge on the subject of Freemasonry and its origin and concepts." He is correct in pointing out that much still needs to be done in the effort to develop a "total picture of the origin of Freemasonry." He is also correct in his conviction that "Prince Hall Freemasonry is more than capable of contributing its share in the development of an overall picture." I encourage him to continue his efforts to bring about the needed changes both in Freemasonry and in Roman Catholicism so that both institutions will be able to contribute more to the uplift of fallen humanity during the upcoming twenty-first century.

The Symbolism of the Cross

by Rev. Dr. Robert L. Uzzel, FPS
(Volume 4, March - 1986)

INTRODUCTION

A symbol has been defined as "something that stands for something else." The same figure may symbolize different things for different people, in different cultures, and during different historical periods. The cross is a symbol quite demonstrative of this fact.

Today, the cross is best known as the symbol of the Christian religion. However, its use as a symbol in religion and mysticism, predates Christianity and, even today, it is a symbol often seen outside the Christian realm.

The great Swiss psychiatrist, Dr. Carl Gustav Jung (1875 - 1961), devoted much of his life to the study of symbols and their relation to the human psyche. In his last book, Man and His Symbols, Jung spoke of the guarded interpretation of the symbolism of the cross when such is found in dreams:

> In the case of a devout Christian, the symbol of the cross can be interpreted only in its Christian context — unless the dream produces a very strong reason to look beyond it. Even then, the specific Christian meaning should be kept in mind. But one cannot say that, at all times and in all circumstances, the symbol of the cross has the same meaning. If that were so, it would be stripped of its numinosity, lose its vitality, and become a mere word.[1]

Jung pointed out that, even in modern conscious experience, the meaning of the cross is extremely varied:

> The cross in the Christian religion, for instance, is a meaningful symbol that expresses a multitude of aspects, ideas and emotions; but a cross after a name on a list, simply indicates that the individual is dead.[2]

In this paper, the writer will seek to explore the varied uses and functions of the cross, both ancient and modern.

THE PRE-CHRISTIAN CROSS

In every part of the world, the cross was used as a religious symbol or ornament long before the Christian era. According to the nineteenth century physician and Masonic writer, Dr. Albert Mackey (1807-1881):

> The symbolism of the cross was in all probability borrowed from usages of antiquity, for from the earliest times and in almost all countries, the cross has been a sacred symbol. It is depicted on the oldest monuments of Egypt, Assyria, Persia and Hindustan...a symbol throughout the Pagan world long previous to its becoming an object of veneration to Christians. In ancient symbology, it was a symbol of eternal life.[3]

On stones dating to the Stone Age is found a solar wheel, consisting of a cross in a circle. This emblem gradually spread all over the world as a religious or magic sign, with few cultures not having some use of the cross.

According to another nineteenth century Masonic writer, General Albert Pike (1809-1891); the serpent upon the cross was the Egyptian standard found on the Grand Staircase of the Temple of Osiris. Pike argued that, on the Pyramid of Ghizeh, there are two kneeling figures erecting a cross, on the top of which is a serpent, and one of the most common emblems on Egyptian monuments is the Crux Ansata (cross with a coiled serpent above it).[4]

The Tau cross was one of the most common of the pre-Christian crosses and was especially common in Egypt. It is so named because of its similarity to the Greek capital letter Tau (T). Pike believed that the Samaritan Tau and the Ethiopian Tavvi were prototypes of the Greek Tau and that, with the Tau representing life and the circle representing eternity, the Tau in a circle represented eternal life.[5]

Another common cross dating to pre-Christian times is the Swastika, which was formed from four Greek capital letters of Gamma (Γ). This has been found on many prehistoric objects in Europe and America. In 1933, the German Nazis adopted it as their official emblem. No doubt many will be surprised to learn that the Nazis merely adopted this ancient symbol—they did not invent it.

According to Pike, both the Hindus and the Celtic Druids built many of their temples in the form of a cross. He cited examples in the Supernal Pagoda at Benares, India and the Druidical subterranean grotto at New Grange, Scotland.[6]

In an article in National Geographic, Professor G. Ernest Wright, archaeologist and Bible scholar, presented a photograph of a "4th century B.C. Persian seal impression, showing a hunter and the cross-like symbol of the Zoroastrian God Ahura-Mazda." Dr. Wright has spent three years with the Crew-McCormick Archaeological Expedition, excavating ruins at Shechem and found this relic with a design similar to that of the Maltese cross.[7]

In the New World, there has been a great deal of interest in the Palenque Cross which has been found among the Mayan Indian relics in southern Mexico, near the Guatemala border. In Time Magazine dated July 7, 1952, a description was given of a temple found and excavated by Dr. Albert Ruz. According to this article, the hidden chamber of the temple was dominated by "the altar, built of two carved stone blocks, and on the altar was a 'Palenque Cross': a stone carving of the Mayan tree of life... Around the Palenque Cross was a ring of human skulls."[8] In an illustrated article in Americas, Professor Linda Schele, of the University of Southern Alabama, spoke of a whole complex of buildings which she designates as the "Group of the Cross" and the "Court of the Cross." She calls this temple the "Temple of Inscriptions" and says,

> ...the primary discovery was a large, unique burial crypt, found under a pyramid. The crypt, among other things, included a large, monolithic sarcophagus with a motif presented on the lid of a falling Maya figure superimposed over a cross element. The cross is constructed of three jeweled (jade) serpents as cross members, supported by a defined chart of the sun god or the god of the north star. The approximate date of the Ruz Tombs is mid-seventh century A.D. by the GMT calculation.[9] The three temples referred to as the Group of the Cross included three structures: The Temples of the Cross, the Foliated Cross and the Sun. Many theories exist as to the meaning of the crosses but quite frankly, no one knows exactly what the meanings of each were.[10]

The fact that these crosses are found only in temples—never in secular buildings—is good evidence that their use was religious. Evidence indicates that these crosses date to the seventh century A.D. Although this is after the time of Christ, there is no evidence that Christianity entered the Western Hemisphere before the Fifteenth Century. Thus, in this sense, these Mayan crosses belong to the pre-Christian era.[11]

CHRISTIAN CROSS

It is believed that Jesus was crucified on a Latin cross, although some insist it was a Tau cross. The Romans used the simple Greek cross, St. Andrew's cross, and the Tau cross (also called St. Anthony's cross). The use of the cross as a symbol of the Christian religion goes back at least to the second century A.D. The early Christian writer, Tertullian, says that the Christians of his time used it daily. St. Augustine wrote about the way early Christians used the cross in performing the sacraments.[12]

As long as Christians were forbidden to display the cross in its true form, they used indications. The fish, the dove, the anchor, the ship and the monogram of Christ, alone or with these, were used as substitutes. Also, Greek letters alpha (α) and omega (ω) were used as substitutes. Doves, birds, and fish represented the faithful. These signs were found on rings, gems, tombstones, lamps and especially in the catacombs. During this period, Egyptian Tau crosses were adopted by the Copts, the first Egyptian Christians.[13]

The Latin cross was favored by the Latin Christians of the West. Its use can be traced to the second half of the second century.[14]

During the Middle Ages, the cross was used at every opportunity. Medieval architects produced crosses in a great variety of designs, many of great beauty. One of the best known was the Calvary Cross, a Latin cross on steps. Standing crosses served various functions, including that of a preaching station. One of the best known of the latter was the Black Friars' cross. Probably the most famous form was the Maltese Cross, used by the Knights of Malta (Hospitallers). This cross contains eight points which represent the eight beatitudes of Matthew 5:3-11, 14. A similar yet somewhat different cross is called the Pattee Cross, meaning the arms are broad and spread at the outer ends. According to Mackey, in 1146, Pope Eugenius III prescribed for the Templars a red cross on their breasts as a symbol of the martyrdom to which they were constantly exposed.[15]

Pike was a student of medieval knighthood and wrote the following:

> Hungus, who in the ninth century, reigned over the Picts in Scotland, is said to have seen in a vision, on a night before a battle, the Apostle St. Andrew, who promised him the victory; and for an assured token thereof, he told him that there should appear over the Pictish host, in the air, such a fashioned cross as he had suffered upon. Hungus awakened, looking up at the sky, saw the promised cross, as did all of both armies, and, Hungus and the Picts, after rendering thanks to the Apostle for their victory, and making their offerings with humble devotion, vowed that from thenceforth, as well as their posterity, and in time of war, would wear a cross of St. Andrew for their badge and cognizance.
>
> Every cross of Knighthood is a symbol of the nine qualities of a Knight of St. Andrew of Scotland, for every order of chivalry required of its votaries, the same virtues and the same excellencies.
>
> Humility, Patience, and Self-Denial are three essential qualities of a Knight of St. Andrew of Scotland. The Cross, sanctified by the blood of the holy ones, who have died upon it; the Cross, which Jesus of Nazareth bore, fainting, along the streets of Jerusalem and up to Calvary, upon which he cried, "Not My Will, O Fa-

ther! but thine be done," is an unmistakable and eloquent symbol of these three virtues. He suffered upon it, because He consorted with and taught the poor and lowly and found His disciples among the fishermen of Galilee and the despised publicans. His life was one of Humility, Patience and Self-Denial.[16]

Aniela Jaffe, a disciple of C.G. Jung, in an article entitled, "Symbolism in the Visual Arts," in Man and His Symbols, gave the following interpretation of the cross in ancient medieval times:

> Up to Carolingian times, the equilateral or Greek cross [magic circle] was the usual form, and therefore the mandala was indirectly implied. But in the course of time, the center moved upward until the cross took on the Latin form, with the stake and the crossbeam, that is customary today. This development is important because it corresponds to the inward development of Christianity up to the high Middle Ages. In simple terms, it symbolized the tendency to remove the center of man and his faith from the earth and to "elevate" it into the spiritual sphere. This tendency sprang from the desire to put into action Christ's saying: "My kingdom is not of this world." Earthly life, the work, and the body were, therefore, forces that had to be overcome. Medieval man's hopes were thus directed to the beyond, for it was only from paradise that the promise of fulfillment beckoned.
>
> This endeavor reached its climax in the Middle Ages and in medieval mysticism. The hopes of the beyond found expression not only in the raising of the center of the cross; it can also be seen in the increasing height of the Gothic cathedrals, which seem to set the laws of gravity at defiance. Their cruciform ground plan is that of the elongated Latin cross (though the baptisteries, with the font in the center, having a true mandala ground plan).
>
> In spite of the far-reaching changes in art, philosophy, and science brought about by the Renaissance, the central symbol of Christianity remained unchanged. Christ was still represented on the Latin cross, as he is today. That meant that the center of religious man remained anchored on a higher, more spiritual plane than that of earthly man, who turned back to nature.[17]

ALCHEMICAL CROSS

The cross figured prominently in another movement which flourished during the Middle Ages – Alchemy.[18] In his magnificent work, Psychology and Alchemy, Jung wrote:

> While dogmas of the Church offered analogies to the alchemical process, these analogies, in strict contrast to alchemy, had become detached from the world of nature through their connection with the historical figure of the Redeemer. The

alchemical 4 in 1, the philosophical gold, the lapis angularis, the agua divina, became, in the Church, the four-armed cross on which the Only-Begotten had sacrificed himself once in history, and at the same time for all eternity. The alchemists ran counter to the Church in preferring to seek knowledge rather than to find through faith, though as medieval people they never thought of themselves as anything but good Christians.[19]

In the same work, Jung further stated:

> The number...probably explains the universal incidence and magical significance of the cross or the circle divided into four. In the present case, the point seems to be to capture and regulate the animal instincts so as to exorcise the danger of falling into unconsciousness.[20]

In another work on the same subject, Jung declared:

> The idea of the cross points beyond simple antithesis to double antithesis, in other words, to a quaternity. To the mind of the alchemist, this meant primarily the intercrossing elements:

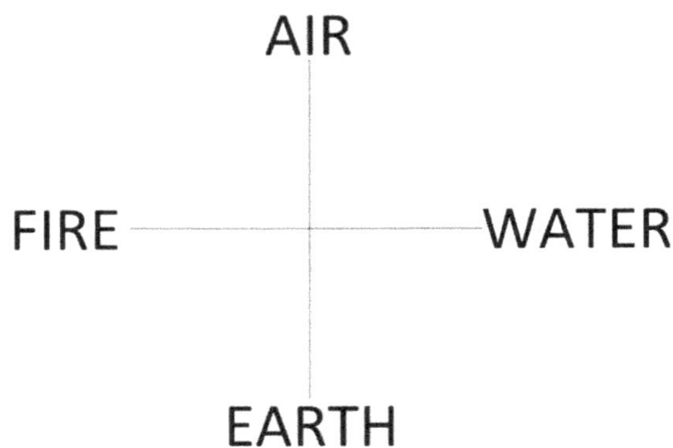

> or the four qualities:

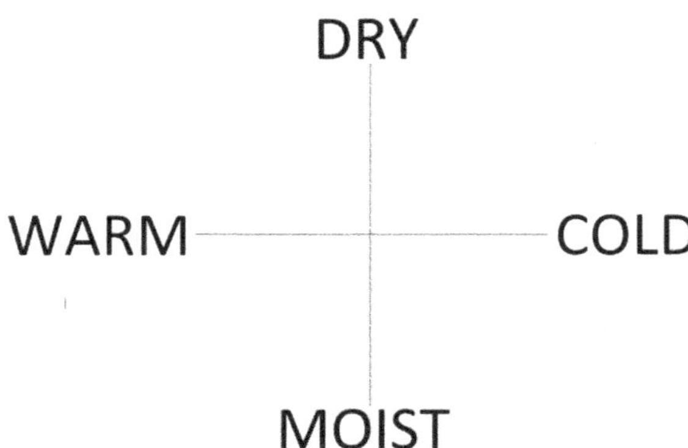

> We know that this fastening to cross denotes a painful state of suspension, or tearing asunder in four directions. The alchemists set themselves the task of rec-

onciling the elements and reducing them to unity.[21]

THE CROSS IN ROSICRUCIANISM

The cross plays a prominent role in the secret society known as Rosicrucianism.[22] In Psychology and Alchemy, Jung commented on this movement:

> Now we know that the regression to the Helios of antiquity, vainly attempted by Julian the Apostate, was succeeded in the Middle Ages by another movement that was expressed in the formula "per crucem and rosam" (through the cross to the rose), which was later condensed into the "Rosie Cross" of the Rosicrucians. Here the essence of the heavenly soul descends into the flower — earth's answer to the sun's countenance. The solar quality has survived in the symbol of the "golden flower" of Chinese alchemy.[23]

According to Albert Pike, the Egyptians saw the cross as the symbol of life and the rose as the symbol of the dawn. Thus, he said, the rose combined with the cross symbolizes the dawn of eternal life.[24] Pike also wrote:

> To unite the Rose to the Cross, was the problem proposed by the High Initiation; and in fact the Occult philosophy being the Universal Synthesis, ought to explain all the phenomena of being.[25]

William J. Whalen, the leading Roman Catholic authority on Freemasonry, in his book, Handbook of Secret Organizations, describes the self-initiation many modern Rosicrucians experience:

> He traces the sign of the cross on the mirror and says, "Hail, O Sacred Symbol of Life, Love and Resurrection. In the center of thy holy body shall come the Rose, the Soul of man's being, and thou shalt be my sign! Hail, Rosy Cross!" He stares at the cross for three minutes.[26]

According to Baptist fundamentalist Walter Martin (who is highly critical of Rosicrucianism and many other movements):

> The cross in Rosicrucianism is the mystical symbol of man's evolutionary development, past, present and future.[27]

THE CROSS IN FREEMASONRY

The cross has played a major role in Freemasonry as well as in Rosicrucianism.[28] However, Mackey insists that this has not always been the case:

> We can find no symbolism of the cross in the primary Degrees of Ancient Craft Masonry. It does not appear among the symbols of the Apprentice, the Fellow Craft, the Maser or the Royal Arch. This is undoubtedly to be attributed to the fact that the cross was considered, by those who invented those Degrees, only in reference to its character as a Christian sign. The subsequent archaeological investigations that have given to the cross a more universal place in iconography were unknown to the old rituals. It is true, that it is referred to, under the name of the rode or rood, in a manuscript of the fourteenth century, published by Halliwell; this was, however, one of the Constitutions of the Operative Freemasons, who were fond of the symbol, and were indebted for it to their ecclesiastical origin, and to their connection with the Gnostics, among whom the cross was a much used symbol. But on the revival in 1717, when the ritual was remodified, and differed very greatly from that meager one in practice among the medieval Freemasons, all allusion to the cross was left out, because the revivalists laid down the principle that the religion of Speculative Freemasonry was not sectarian but universal. And although this principle was in some points, as in the lines parallel, neglected, the reticence as to the Christian sign of salvation has continued to the present day; so that the cross cannot be considered as a symbol in the primary and original Degrees of Freemasonry.
>
> But in the advanced Degrees, the cross has been introduced as an important symbol. In some of them...is to be viewed with reference to its Christian origin and meaning. Thus, in the original Rose Croix and Kadosh—no matter what may be the modern interpretation given to it—it was simply a representation of the cross of Christ. In others of a philosophical character, such as the ineffable Degrees, the symbolism of the cross was in all probability borrowed from the usages of antiquity.[29]

In Morals and Dogma, Pike made numerous references to the cross, stating that reverence for generative power, formed the philosophical cross of the Masons.[30] In his commentary on the 23rd Degree, he stated that the cross within the circle is the light by means whereof chaos developed.[31] In reference to the 32nd Degree, he interprets the cross as symbolic of devotedness and self-sacrifice.[32]

The cross has other Masonic uses, especially in the York Rite, where the medieval orders of Knights of Malta and Knights Templar are resurrected.

THE CROSS IN JUNGIAN PSYCHOLOGY

Carl Gustav Jung devoted much of his life to the study of symbols and their influence on the human psyche, both conscious and unconscious. He believed that symbols were closely related to "archetypes" (primordial images and ideals which are common to all men) and that archetypes compose the "collective unconscious" (the powerful spiritual inheritance of human development, reborn in each individual brain structure). He studied the symbolism of the cross in both Christian and pre-Christian cultures; in the magical science of alchemy, which intrigued him; and in secret societies, which he regarded as a stage on the road to individuation (personal integration). Throughout Jung's voluminous writings, there are numerous references to both Rosicrucianism and Freemasonry.[33]

In his book, Psychological Types, Jung stated:

> The interpretation of the cross as a symbol of divine love is semiotic, because "divine love" describes the fact to be expressed better and more aptly than a cross, which can have many other meanings. On the other hand, an interpretation of the cross is symbolic when it puts the cross beyond all conceivable explanations, regarding it as expressing an as yet unknown and incomprehensible fact of a mystical or transcendent, i.e., psychological, nature, which simply finds itself most appropriately represented in the cross.[34]

In Psychology and Religion: West and East, he further stated:

> The cross signifies order as opposed to the disorderly chaos of the formless multitude. It is, in fact, one of the prime symbols of order, as I have shown elsewhere. In the domain of the psychological processes, it functions as an organizational center, and in states of psychic disorder caused by invasion of unconscious contents, it appears as a mandala divided into four.[35]

In The Symbolic Life, he made the following references to the cross:

> When I went to America to investigate the unconscious of Negroes, I had in mind this particular problem; are these collective patterns recently inherited...A Negro told me a dream in which occurred the figure of a man crucified on a wheel...He was a very uneducated Negro from the South and not particularly intelligent. It would have been most probable, given the well-known religious character of the Negroes, that he should dream a man crucified on a cross. The cross would have been a personal acquisition. But it is rather improbable that he should dream of the man crucified on a wheel that is a very uncommon image. Of course, I cannot prove to you that by some curious chance the Negro had not seen a picture of, or heard something of the sort and then dreamt about it; but if he had not any model for this idea, it would be an archetypal image, because the crucifixion on a wheel is a mythological motif.[36]
>
> The use of a magic circle, or mandala, as it is called in the East, for healing purposes is an archetypal idea.

When a man is ill, the Pueblo Indians of New Mexico make a sand-painting of a mandala with four gates... In Christian symbolism, the totality is Christ, and the healing process consists of the imitation of Christ. The four gates are replaced by four arms of the cross.[37]

CURRENT USES OF THE CROSS

Today, forms of the cross appear on the flags of many nations, including Great Britain's Union Jack, which contains the English Cross of St. George (a red cross on a white background), the Scottish Cross of St. Andrew (a diagonal white cross on a blue background), and the Irish Cross of St. Patrick (a diagonal red cross on a white background). The Red Cross (a simple, red Greek cross on a white background) is a symbol of work done as a Christian act, with red signifying valor and bravery and white signifying purity.[38]

On a church altar, a cross symbolizes Christ's atonement. A cross worn on a chain around the neck is called a pectoral cross (from the Latin word "pectralis," which means "of the heart"). The cross rests over the heart. Originally, it was worn only by a bishop. Today it is worn by clergy and laity alike. A pendant cross is suspended in a church sanctuary. A processional cross is attached to a staff and carried at the head of an ecclesiastical procession. A rood cross is placed at the center of a rood beam, which is suspended from wall to wall at a church entrance. This indicates that entrance to heaven must be via the cross of Christ. A spire cross is placed at the top of a church steeple to proclaim to all the surrounding community that Jesus is the highest of the high.[39]

CONCLUSIONS

From ancient times to the modern world, the cross has been a symbol in various cultures. Truly its usage is universal. The writer is a Christian minister, Prince Hall Freemason, and avid reader of the works of C.G. Jung. Regardless of which of these three "hats" he is wearing at the moment, the cross is significant. He hopes members of Lux e Tenebris will find the reading of this paper as interesting as the research and writing were for him.

REFERENCES

[1]Carl Gustav Jung, ed., Man and His Symbols, (New York: Dell Publishing Company, Inc., 1964, 87).

[2]Ibid, 81.

[3]Albert Mackey, Encyclopedia of Freemasonry, Vol. 1, (Chicago, Illinois: Masonic History Company, 1929), 252.

[4] Albert Pike, Morals and Dogmas of the Ancient and Accepted Scottish Rite of Freemasonry (Washington, D.C.: Supreme Council of the Southern Jurisdiction, A.A.S.R.U.S.A., 1950), 502.

[5]Ibid, 503-5.

[6]Ibid, 505.

[7]G. Ernest Wright, The Last Thousand Years Before Christ," National Geographic, December 1960.

[8]Time, 7 July 1952.

[9]Linda Schele, "Space and Life Style—A Maya Answer," Americas, May 1973.

[10]Ibid.

[11]Alex Horne, The Pre-Christian Cross," The New Age, April 1974, 44.

[12]Johannes Troyer, The Cross as Symbol and Ornament (Philadelphia: Westminster Press, 1981), 29.

[13]Ibid.

[14]Ibid, 41.

[15]Mackey, 253.

[16]Pike, 801-2.

[17]Jung, Man and His Symbols, 273-5.

[18]Alchemy was a primitive form of chemistry. For centuries, the alchemists

worked diligently in laboratories seeking the transformation of base metals into gold and the discovery of the elixir of life. Yet this magical science also had a spiritual dimension. Jung found in alchemy much that was relevant to psychic transformation and the modern psychology of the unconscious.

[19]Carl Gustav Jung, Psychology and Alchemy (Princeton, New Jersey: Princeton University Press, 1968), 35.

[20]Ibid, 150.

[21]Carl Gustav Jung, Mysterium Conjunctionis: An Inquiry into the Separation and Synthesis of Psychic Opposites in Alchemy (Princeton, New Jersey: Princeton University Press, 1970), 421-2.

[22]One of the founders of Rosicrucianism was Michael Meier (1568-1622), a well-known alchemist. At present, there are at least four Rosicrucian organizations in the United States. The largest of these is the Ancient Mystical Order Rosae Crucis (A.M.O.R.C.), headquartered in San Jose, California. Such modern operations have little if any connection with original Rosicrucianism.

[23]Jung, Psychology and Alchemy, 76.

[24]Pike, 291.

[25]Ibid, 821-2.

[26]William J. Whalen, Handbook of Secret Organizations (Milwaukee, Wisconsin: Bruce Publishing Company, 1966), 143. Some Rosicrucians belong to local lodges but the vast majority initiate themselves via mail-order materials. This organization spends huge sums of money on advertising each year.

[27]Walter Martin, The Kingdom of the Cults (Minneapolis, Minnesota: Bethany Fellowship, Inc., 1965), 428.

[28]Some scholars believe that there is a historical connection between Freemasonry and Rosicrucianism, as indicated by the Chapter of Rose Croix (degrees 15-18) in Scottish Rite Masonry. Today, the two organizations have no direct connection.

[29]Mackey, 252.

[30]Pike, 771.

[31]Ibid, 782.

[32]Ibid, 854.

[33]While Jung himself was not a Mason, the order definitely influenced his life and thought. His grandfather, who like him, was a Doctor of Medicine and whose name was also Carl Gustav Jung, was at one time Grand Master of Masons in Switzerland. Throughout his life, Jung was intrigued by a rumor (with little basis to be believed) that his grandfather was the illegitimate son of Johann Wolfgang von Goethe, who was also a Freemason. Jung was deeply influenced by Goethe's Faust. Carl Gustav Jung, Memories, Dreams, Reflections (New York: Random House, Inc., 1965), 232.

[34]Carl Gustav Jung, Psychological Types (Princeton, New Jersey: Princeton University Press, 1971), 217.

[35]Carl Gustav Jung, Psychology and Religion: West and East (Princeton, New Jersey: Princeton University Press, 1969), 284.

[36]Carl Gustav Jung, The Symbolic Life: Miscellaneous Writings (Princeton, New Jersey: Princeton University Press, 1976), 38-9. Jung wrote a number of articles on Black psychology. On one trip to the United States, he was given a shave and haircut by a Black barber in Chattanooga, Tennessee. Later, while visiting an African village, he awoke startled from a dream of this same barber applying a curling iron to his hair.

[37]Ibid, 123.

[38]Loice Gouker, Dictionary of Church Terms and Symbols (Norwalk, Connecticut: C.R. Gibson Company, 1964), 24.

[39]Ibid.

COMMENTS

Brother Gean O. Taylor, M.P.S. writes:

A rare and diversified look into the various meanings and symbolisms of the cross. In the introduction, the writer gives the definition of a symbol as, "something that stands for something else." I have always been more partial toward "a sensible image used to express a hidden meaning."

I enjoyed the writing itself and it gives an interesting insight into the cross from both a Christian standpoint, as well as a Prince Hall Freemason's standpoint. The references are clearly outlined as they should be, and are well known to Masonic scholars around the world. This manuscript will be enjoyed by all who read it as it has something of interest for both the Ancient Craft Mason and the Scottish Rite Mason alike.

Brother Joseph A. Walkes, Jr., F.P.S. writes:

I want to thank Reverend Bro. Robert L. Uzzel, F.P.S. for a most fascinating paper and a subject that I had never given too much thought to. Of course, Bro. Uzzel being a minister, would have automatically been drawn to this subject "The Symbolism of the Cross." I must say in all honesty, his paper forced me into the books.

There is however, one weakness in Bro. Uzzel's paper, and I would like, to use Bro. Winston O. Williams, M.P.S.'s term, to "piggy back" on Bro. Uzzel's thought provoking paper. The weakness I found was a lack of illustrations. For with the appropriate illustrations, the viewer, while reading the paper, would have a far better understanding of the subject. I have used three works to help me "Mackey's Revised Encyclopedia of Freemasonry," by Albert G. Mackey (New York, Macoy Publishing and Masonic Supply Co., Inc., 1966), pp. 253-254; "Freemasons' Guide and Compendium," by Bernard E. Jones (London, George G. Harrap & Co., Ltd., 1953), pp. 119; 289-290; 354 and 480; and, "A New Encyclopedia of Freemasonry," by Arthur Edward White (New York, Weathervane Books, 1970) pp. 158-159.

In order to better understand Bro. Uzzel's paper, a look at the crosses is in order:

JERUSALEM CROSS

A Greek cross between four crosslets. It was adopted by Baldwyn as the arms of the Kingdom of Jerusalem, and has since been deemed a symbol of the Holy Land. It is also the jewel of the Knights of the Holy Sepulcher. Symbolically, the four small crosses typify the four wounds of the Savior in the hands and feet, and the large central cross shows forth his death for that world to which the four extremities point.

MALTESE CROSS

A cross of eight points, worn by the Knights of Malta. It is heraldically described as "a cross pattee," but the extremity of each pattee notched at a deep angle. The eight points are said to refer symbolically to the eight beatitudes. (See Matthew v, 3 to 11).

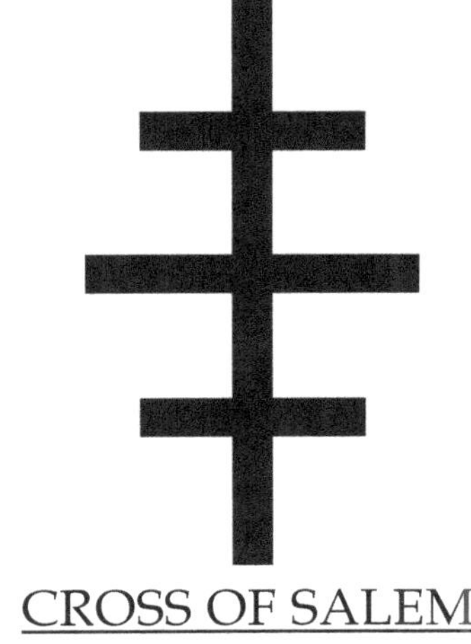

CROSS OF SALEM

Also called the Pontifical Cross, because it is borne before the Pope. It is a cross, the upright being crossed by three lines, the upper and lower shorter than the middle one. It is the insignia of the Grand Master and Past Grand Masters of th Grand Encampment of Knights Templar of the United States. The same cross placed on a slant is the insignia of the Sovereign Grand Commander of the United Supreme Council of the Ancient and Accepted Scottish Rite.

PASSION CROSS

The cross on which Jesus suffered crucifixion. It is the most common form of the cross. When rayonnani, or having rays issuing from the point of intersection of the limbs, it is the insignia of the Commander of a Commandery of Knights Templar, according to the American System.

PATRIARCHAL CROSS

A cross, the upright piece being twice crossed, the upper arms shorter than the lower. It is so called because it is borne before the patriarch in the Roman Church. It is the insignia of the officers of Grand Encampment of Knights Templar of the United States. The same cross placed on a slant is the insignia of all possessors of the Thirty-third Degree in the Ancient and Accepted Scottish Rite.

SAINT ANDREW'S CROSS

A saltier or cross whose decussation or crossing of the arms is in the form of the letter X. Said to be the form of cross on which Saint Andrew suffered martyrdom. As he is the patron saint of Scotland, the Saint Andrew's cross forms part of the jewel of the Grand Master of the Grand Lodge of Scotland, which is "a star set with brilliants having in the center a field azure (blue), charged with Saint Andrew on the Cross, gold; this is pendant from the upper band of the collar, while from the lower band is pendant the jewel proper, the Compasses extended, with the Square and Segment of a Circle of 90°; the points of the Compasses resting on the Segment, and in the center, the sun between the Square and Compasses." The Saint Andrew's cross is also the jewel of the Twenty-ninth Degree of the Ancient and Accepted Scottish Rite, or Grand Scottish Knight of Saint Andrew.

TAU CROSS

The cross on which Saint Anthony is said to have suffered martyrdom. It is in the form of the letter "T".

TEMPLAR CROSS

Andre Favin, a French heraldic writer, says that the original badge of the Knights Templar was a Patriarchal Cross, and Clarke, in his History of Knighthood, makes the same statement, but this is in error. At first, the Templars wore a white mantle without any cross. But in 1146, Pope Eugenius III prescribed for them a red cross on their breast, as a symbol of the martyrdom to which they were constantly exposed. The cross of the Hospitallers was white on a black mantle, and that of the Templars was different in color but of the same form, namely the outer ends. In this it differed from the true Maltese Cross, worn by the Knights of Malta, which was a cross pattee, the limbs deeply notched so as to make a cross of eight points. Sir Walter Scott, with his not unusual heraldic inaccuracy, and Godfrey Higgins, who is not often inaccurate, but only fanciful at times, both describe the Templar cross as having eight points, thus confounding it with the Cross of Malta. In the statutes of the Order of the Temple, the cross prescribed is that depicted in the Charter of Transmission, and is a cross pattee.

TEUTONIC CROSS

The cross formerly worn by the Teutonic Knights. It is described in heraldry as "a cross potent, sable (or black), charged with another cross double potent (or gold), and surcharged with an escutcheon argent (or silver), bearing a double-headed eagle sable (or black)." It has been adopted as the jewel of the Kadosh of the Ancient and Accepted Scottish Rite in the United States, but the original jewel of the degree was a Latin or Passion Cross.

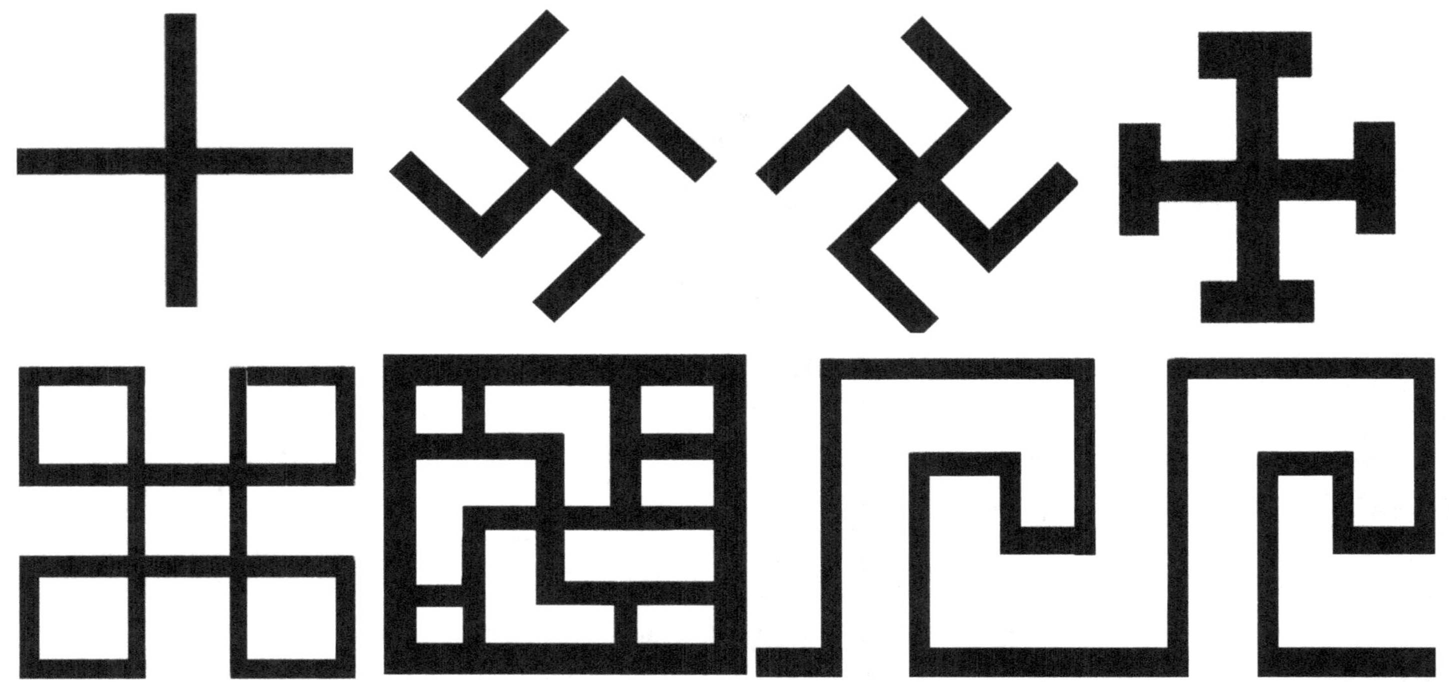

These figures show the Cross and its development into various forms of the swastika (fylfot) and similar devices, most of them demonstrating the Cardinal Points.

CARDINAL

We speak in Freemasonry of cardinal virtues, cardinal points and cardinal sins. Briefly, this curious word means "important, significant" and carries with it a mental image of matters of great moment, all revolving around a center point acting as a hinge, or pivot (Latin, cardo). Much ecclesiastical history is wrapped up in this word, which is associated with the red color of the robe worn by the Roman Catholic cardinal—that is, worn by a powerful priest occupying a fundamentally important place. We go to the doors made and hung by the ancient peoples for the original idea of the meaning of the word. There are two vertical pins, or dowels, projecting from the door, one from the top and one from the bottom, each fitting into a socket, and on these pivots the door swung. The ancients took this hinged door as a figure, or symbol, and supposed that at the top of the universe was a pivot upon which the heavens revolved, while at the bottom was another pivot, corresponding to that at the bottom of the door.

In the course of time, the old Roman writers applied the word "cardinal" to the four points east, west, north and south, and to the winds blowing from those quarters. The east symbolizes wisdom; west, strength; north, darkness; and south, beauty. We are told that the cardinal — that is, the most important virtues in Masonry—are prudence, temperance, fortitude, and justice; the first to direct, the second to chasten, and the third to support a Brother, while the fourth should be a guide to all his actions. But the Initiate is also taught the high place occupied by other excellencies of character—secrecy, fidelity, and obedience—of which the ritual offers a full explanation.

The cross is an image of the cardinal points, and has been so from long before Christian days; in particular, the swastika form of cross, the fylfot, commonly regarded as a good luck charm. The name swastika derives from the Sanskrit word meaning "well being." The "true" swastika indicates the sunwise direction or "sacred circuit," the "false" one (curiously, the one debased by its adoption as a Nazi symbol), the anti-sunwise direction.

CRUCIFORM LODGES

There is a possibility that some of the early Lodges may have been cruciform in arrangement. Reliable evidence on the point is lacking, but there are students who believe that in some cases, Lodges were of this pattern, impracticable though it would appear to be with regard to the ceremonies with which we are familiar. It may be that, if they were cruciform Lodges, they consisted of inner Lodges denoted by floor lines, within which certain parts of the ceremony were worked.

WHEN DRINKING A MASONIC TOAST

The significant movement of hand and glass, which reminds every Entered Apprentice of a communication made to him by the Master of the Lodge, soon after the light dawned upon him, was possibly suggested by the common custom at one time of making the sign of the Cross over the glass of wine...

LUX

According to Hook's Church Dictionary, the figure of the cross "exhibits at the same time the three letters in the word Lux" (Light).

CROSS SYMBOLISM

The Calvary Cross folds up as a double cube, and that cube can open only as a cross. In the science of the mystics, an eloquent symbolism arises out of this fact, and it is not without analogies in Masonry, though I am not intending to press them, because things which belong to one another in different schools of thought must not be confused with one another on the basis of their spiritual affinity. The Altar of every Christian Temple is in the form of a double cube laid sidewise, and this would open as a cross resting horizontally on the ground, being the position of the Calvary Cross—according to tradition—when Christ was nailed thereon. The Holy Sacrifice of the Mass offered on the Altar is a memorial of this Divine Event. On such an Altar does the soul of every man in responding to the call of God offer up itself in sacrifice. But the Altar under another aspect represents the universe, and the sacred things which ought always to be laid within it signify the Divine Immanence in creation. When the cubical Altar of the universe opens as a cosmic cross, God immanent becomes God manifest.

In the sense of the microcosm, the double cube is the body of man, having a divine nature hidden within it. The opening of this cube is the passage of latent into active and manifest divinity by the crucifixion of the evil within us. Every Masonic Temple, when properly arranged, is in the form of an oblong square, which is laid sidewise. We know that it represents the universe, and the sacred work which takes place therein corresponds to Divine Activity in the cosmos. Such a cube is symbolical also of the Craft Grades, and it opens in the High Christian Grades as the Cross of Christ.

Once again, my thanks to Reverend Bro. Robert L. Uzzel for a most fascinating paper.

Bro. Brian L. Abrams writes:

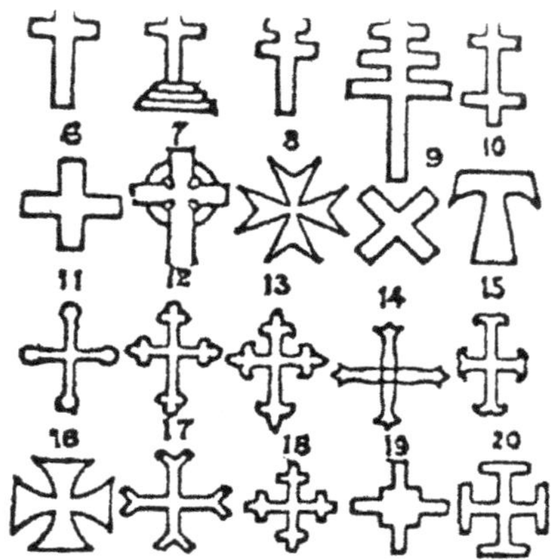

Cross. 1 Latin; 2 Calvary; 3 Patriarchal or Archiepiscopal; 4 Papal; 5 Lorraine; 6 Greek; 7 Celtic; 8 Maltese; 9 St. Andrew's; 10 Tau; 11 Pommée; 12 Botonée; 13 Pattée; 14 Avellan; 15 Moline; 16 Formée; 17 Fourchée; 18 Crosslet; 19 Quadrate; 20 Potent (Jerusalem). See also ANKH, SWASTIKA, *Illustr.*

I am impressed with the research of Rev. Bro. Uzzel, as I have been reading other works of his. The compiled information on the origins and usages of the cross as a symbol is interesting and informative. In reference to Gen. Albert Pike's "Morals and Dogmas" description of the Egyptian standard, found on the staircase of the temple of Osiris, that had a Serpent upon the Cross, there are modern day variations of the same, used in the military, especially those that identify the medical corps.

Medical Corps

Dental Corps

It was also reported that the Crux Ansata (A.K.A. the Egyptian Ankh) was one of the most common emblems on Egyptian monuments. Viewing the Ankh we see that the Greek Tau Cross, the nineteenth letter of the Greek alphabet, is an integral part of it, but with a loop or reported coiled Serpent above it. At first, it was an extrinsic view, I imagined, when reading of the Crux Ansata; after viewing groups of pictorial likeness of crosses, the thought came to mind that the coiled Serpent may not have been intended as such and may have been a circle instead! A circle representing 360 degrees or eternity, therefore, the Ankh would have an extrinsic meaning of eternal life.

The Japanese Torii, which forms the gateways to the Shinto Temples, is also interesting in its construction.

The lower portion of two vertical columns with a bar across their tops could be representative of the 16th letter of the Greek alphabet π = Pi, which mathematically denotes the ratio of the circumference of a circle or 360°, supporting what could with a bit of poetic license be a Roman number III (3). Symbolically, the two of them together could be interpreted as:

1 2 3

(A)
(1) Fire
(2) Water
(3) Air

(B)
(1) God the Father
(2) The Son Imposed Upon π = Pi or 360°
(3) The Holy Spirit

Together indicating Life Eternal.

The Greek-letter symbolic meanings, have been considered because of the "Septuaginta" (seventy), the Greek version (translation) of the Hebrew Old Testament. Legend has it that seventy emissaries from Jerusalem made it for Ptolemy about 270 B.C. (Webster Collegiate Dictionary, 5th ed., p.207).

Masonic symbolism in its interpretations are not immune to the different schools of thought, nor as it was mentioned on pages 1 and 2 of the work we are commenting on, are the various crosses. Rev. Bro. Uzzel is first a Minister of the teaching A.M.E. Church, and has much to offer. Thank you Bro. Uzzel for the "Symbolism of the Cross." It answered some questions for me.

Do Prince Hall Masons Need A Handbook of Freemasonry

by Honorable Floyd L. Bass, MPS (Conn.)

A MASONIC VADE MECUM
(A Review by Harry A. Williamson, and Harold V. B. Voorhis)
(4th Edition, March 1986)

This "Masonic Vade Mecum," a manual or a book for ready reference, produced a fair amount of heat along with a good measure of Masonic "light" during a long hot summer fifty years ago, in the columns of "Masonic Notes" by Mertram L. Baker in The New York Age. The two internationally recognized Masonic historians, Williamson and Voorhis, praised the Right Worshipful Grand Lecturer of the Most Worshipful Prince Hall Grand Lodge of F & AM of Missouri, Brother B. F. Adams, for his scholarship in the preparation of such a "handbook" for use in the Grand Lodge Schools of Instruction in that jurisdiction. Each also took Brother Adams to task because of some errors of judgment and of fact, and Voorhis, who had critiqued an earlier work by Adams, relied on the review by Williamson of "Masonic Vade Mecum" as the basis for his own contribution. This public acknowledgment of the mutual respect and admiration between two Masonic scholars, Voorhis for Williamson, comes as no surprise to members of the Craft, yet it undergirds the usefulness of a well-researched "MANUAL" for Grand Lodge, Grand Chapter, Grand Council and Grand Commandery "SCHOOLS OF INSTRUCTION" at the present time.

"Masonic Vade Mecum," A Review by Harry A. Williamson: The above represents the title of a booklet of about 92 pages, divided into several chapters, compiled by Brother B.F. Adams, Grand Lecturer of the Grand Lodge, F & AM of Missouri (Prince Hall), and while it does not carry the imprint of that grand body, it is evidently published with its sanction since the volume is offered for distribution through the office of the Grand Secretary. One of the suitable definitions of the title reads, "Go With Me," and one is amply satisfied with the journey when he reaches the conclusion. A careful study of the contents should prove of great benefit to some of our so-called "big Masons," and in the end, they will no doubt come to realize the extent of their ignorance concerning the Craft. I do heartily recommend this volume, particularly to those elements in the Fraternity whom I classify as "book Masons, ritual parrots and emblem wearers."

In his Preface, the author sets out the object of his work and in part, says: "A careful study of the contents will, I am quite sure, make every Brother who reads it, a bright Mason." To which I add, Amen.

Chapter I, contains about 13 subdivisions under appropriate titles:

(1) In outlining Speculative Masonry, references are made to moral and religious doctrines, a belief in God, immortality, and philosophical doctrines. A statement reads that such are to be found in the "Higher Degrees" of the Craft. Just what is intended I do not clearly understand, but presume the author means those doctrines are further developed in both understanding and beauty in the degrees of some of the concordant orders, since Ancient Craft Masonry comprises but three degrees.

(2) A comprehensive study of our Institution in connection with the Holy Bible is recommended and quite a list of Biblical references are furnished for the purpose.

(3) A brief statement of the origin of the jurisdiction of Missouri is presented. Upon this subject, "another authority" is referred to, but the author makes a serious error in failing to give the name of this other authority, and the title of his work. Unless the sources of statements of that character are given, they do not possess any historical value whatever because the student requires facts and not generalities. The reader obtains bare information of the existence of a Masonic Home maintained at Hannibal, with 26 inmates, but that is all.

(4) Under the caption of "Why the W.M. Wears a Hat," three reasons are cited. I might add another surrounding the custom, and its origin, in the fact that during the very early years that monks whose heads are always or most always covered with a cap, were active members of the Craft, and because of their learning, were generally selected to preside over the various assemblies of the brethren when held from time to time.

(5) Here follow brief notes pertaining to the ritual, the symbols of both the Entered Apprentice and Fellow Craft degrees, the "Twelve Original

Points" and the benefits to be derived through membership.

The most important features of Chapter II comprises a definition of Freemasonry, ten commandments for the Senior Warden, the rights and powers of a Lodge, and the significance of the apron. In this chapter, the author endeavors to explain the reason for the use of "A.F. & A.M." in the title in some of the American jurisdictions, and so far as its use by either the Caucasian and Prince Hall bodies are concerned, the information given is neither clear nor accurate.

The original Grand Lodge of England, the body that erected African Lodge No. 459 at Boston, Massachusetts in the 18th century, incorporated the phrase "Free and Accepted Masons" in its title. The so called Athol Grand Lodge, formed some 27 years later by dissenters from the original organization made use of "Ancient, Free and Accepted Masons." Now, it must be clearly borne in mind that the latter body did not, at any time prior to the consolidation of both groups in 1813, create a constituency in which membership was confined exclusively or in part of black men, consequently from that point of view and from either a technical or Masonic legal standpoint, the Prince Hall bodies ought not to make use of any other phrases in their titles than "Free and Accepted Masons." The greater portion of the Caucasian American Grand Lodges are descendants of the "Ancient" Grand Lodge of England, and while I have not at this time examined the records, feel positive that not more than two are directly descended from the original jurisdiction while one or two may trace their origin to Scotland.

Chapter III, is devoted almost exclusively to ritualistic explanations, questions and answers. However, the first sub-heading is, "Masonic Notes of Interest," and in one portion quotes from "The Northern Freemason" (English), November, 1933, relative to natives being denied admission as members or visitors in Lodges in Africa.

I doubt the accuracy of the statement appearing in that periodical because, in both Nigeria and on the Gold Coast, natives have been admitted into Lodges both as members and visitors for very many years; several of such mixed and native Lodges are very well up to the register of the Grand Lodge of England. My sources of information are two: The "annual" issued by the International Masonic Association at Geneva, Switzerland, and photographs, etc., of the membership of at least six Gold Coast Lodges, mixed and native. These photographs, programs, etc., were sent to me by a native African Freemason with whom I have held a regular correspondence for many years.

There is one Lodge out there, the name and number of which has escaped me for the moment, in which only men whose annual income must exceed $40,000.00, are eligible for membership, and few men, Europeans, mixed African or natives, ever visit for that reason.

In Chapter III, mention is also made of the existence of three Lodges on the North American Continent whose membership, while confined exclusively to Negroes, the Lodges belong to Caucasian grand jurisdictions namely: Union Lodge No. 18, at Halifax, Nova Scotia; Alpha No. 116, at Newark, NJ; and Thistle No. 1003, at Panama; the latter belonging to the Grand Lodge of Scotland, the others to the bodies in their respective territories. Brother Adams ought to have stated from whom he procured that information and in this matter, I am presuming to take the credit of discovering the existence of the first and third of the three mentioned. The results of my research was published some eight or more years ago in the columns of the late National Fraternal Review, formerly located at Chicago, Illinois, of which Victor A. Thompson, now Grand Secretary of Illinois, was the editor. It has frequently happened that some of my research is published from time to time by various writers without due credit being given to me.

Chapter IV, elaborates upon the historical side of certain ceremonies, etc., also about ancient Hebrew history. These features I do not feel sufficiently qualified to comment upon. If any of this matter is original research or quoted from various writers, the author fails to state. He gives some space and not quite enough to the subject of Hiram Abiff. It is, indeed, unfortunate that Brother Adams did not have access to a copy of "Who Was Hiram Abiff," by J.S.M. Ward, London, 1925, before preparing this portion of his booklet, for he would have found the volume referred to, both interesting and informative upon the subject. Brother Adams also refers to four well-known Caucasian Americans, who had been made Freemasons "at sight." Careful research would have revealed the fact that there have been about twenty-five made under that prerogative of a Grand Master: why did he not mention at least one member of our race, who received such an honor, the late Dr. Booker T. Washington, who was made "at sight" by Massachusetts. In the files of "The Builder" of St. Louis, Missouri (now defunct), data relative to the identity of the Caucasians can be procured.

We will pass over Chapter V, which treats with the poetic and religious features of Freemasonry: the Templars, Landmarks, etc., and comment upon a portion of Chapter VI, in which the author discusses the regularity of Negro Masonry. First, or rather may I suggest to the author, that in the future, refrain from making use of the numerals of 32° when writing upon Ancient Craft Masonry because there is no such degree in the Fraternity. I have attained that degree in the Scottish Rite of Freemasonry, but at no time in any of my work, have I ever combined membership in Symbolic Masonry and the Scottish Rite, when discussing the former. Critical writers do not deem such practice as being in good taste. Further in this chapter, its author says that Union Lodge No. 18 at Halifax, previously referred to, belongs to the Grand Lodge of England. That statement is not correct. It was originally founded by that body, but is now upon the register of the Grand Lodge of Nova Scotia, as an examination of any of the proceedings of that body will reveal. Brother Adams seems not to appreciate Alpha No. 116, Thistle No. 1013, and Union No. 18, because they are composed exclusively of black men, and are not classified as "clandestine" by other grand jurisdictions throughout the world. The reason is very simple; those Lodges belong to jurisdictions that are "officially" recognized by all the other Grand Lodges, while the Prince Hall organizations are "not officially" recognized by the same groups.

In this same chapter, the author has introduced the Order of the Eastern Star. Why this has been done, I am unable to understand, for he ought to realize there is absolutely no relationship between Symbolic Masonry and that Order; the former is extraneous in every sense of the word, and purely an American contraption. I admit that association has been of much benefit to its members, and indirectly of great help to the Craft in numerous ways, but it must not be identified in any manner with Ancient Craft Masonry. In many of the Caucasian American jurisdictions, that order is forbidden to use Masonic Halls for its meetings; in Pennsylvania, Freemasons are prohibited membership in the Order under penalty of expulsion, and the same rule is very rigidly enforced among the Lodges belonging to the Grand Lodge of England, throughout the world, and in recent years, the Grand Lodge of Scotland planned similar legislation. Numerous American writers have, without success, endeavored to create an intimate connection between the American Order of the Eastern Star and the Adoptive Lodges which flourished in Europe during the 18th and early 19th centuries.

Other than the exceptions noted herewith, the "Masonic Vade Mecum" is indeed a volume worth the while.

The foregoing review by Harry A. Williamson of the "Masonic Vade Mecum," by B.F. Adams, was circulated in Bertram L. Baker's column, "Masonic Notes," in the July 20 and July 27, 1935 issues of The New York Age. The mere suggestion that this thorough-going critique stimulated the readership of both members of the Craft and laypersons, is something of an understatement. There is a phrase from the African folklore that, "when the elephants fight, the grass gets trampled." There is also another expression that "authors cannot afford to be critics, and critics should never become authors." The following contribution by another Masonic titan, exemplifies both of the comments. The Masonic historian from the white, New Jersey Constitution, Harold Van Buren Voorhis, reviewed Harry A. Williamson's review of a "Masonic Vade Mecum" as follows:

> The review of a "Masonic Vade Mecum" by my good friend, Harry A. Williamson, in your columns, interested me very much. Although I have not seen the volume, though one has been ordered, I am convinced that it is worthwhile—mainly because Bro. Williamson says so.
>
> It must be borne in mind, that in writing on subjects such as covered by both the book itself and the review, items creep in, which are both extraneous and sometimes not true to fact. This is because of the many angles reached by the detailed treatment, many of which are not complete in themselves. As new information and data are being turned up all the time, views expressed are often out of date by the time the printing occurs.
>
> In order to correct a statement or two, made by Bro. Williamson, I write the following without comment. I know he dislikes misinformation and when, through some lack of data he, like all of us, falls into the pit, so to speak, he is the first to acknowledge it. He knows I am the same way and hence, I feel free to comment directly upon this subject.
>
> In the October number of "The Square and Compass," (Denver, Col.) for 1934, there appeared an article concerning Colored Masonry by a B.F. Adams, grand lecturer for Colored Masons in Missouri. In this article, several statements were made covering the very items now brought out in his book. I answered the article in the January, 1935 number, but apparently Bro. Adams did not take my reply as seriously as he might have done, because he has made the very errors in his book, which Bro. Williamson reviewed. The latter brother has seen neither the original article by Bro. Adams nor my reply, but he criticized the very same points, in the main, as I had done formerly. What I wish to mention here, as the whole reply did not relate to matters discussed in the review, is the part pertaining to the three lodges of colored men mentioned, as a point to prove inter-visitation. I quote directly from my original answer:
>
>> So far the illustrations of Negro lodges given in the article in question are concerned, two are outside of the United States and have no concern in this discussion. The other (Alpha No. 116, New Jersey, in which I have sat) may be mentioned in truthfulness as the writer has done, but so far as the members are concerned, their Masonic activity consists of going to their own

Lodge (with rare exceptions), attending Grand Lodge of Instruction once a year, and Grand Lodge once a year.

One of the others, No. 18, is not in existence. In 1855, five colored men were initiated into Royal Sussex Lodge No. 6, R.S.N.M. They subsequently applied to the Hon. Alexander Keith, the District Grand Master of the District Grand Lodge of England, in Nova Scotia, for a dispensation. This was granted and a charter was issued on December 3, 1856, by the Grand Lodge of England, numbered 994. The number was changed to 693 in 1863. The Lodge joined the Grand Lodge of Nova Scotia in 1869, and was assigned the number 18. For many years it did good work, when it was in the hands of capable brethren, and they confined their candidates to men of color in Nova Scotia. However, in 1910, they accepted petitions from men of their race no matter where they resided, i.e., in British Columbia, other parts of Canada, and, at times, the United States.

Soon after this, the secretary became short in his accounts and the minutes were not properly kept with the results that, after investigation, the Grand Lodge took up the Charter in June 1916, and the Lodge has not functioned since.

The members in good standing were given demits at large. One or two brethren affiliated with other Lodges, but it was difficult for them to get in.

The thought must not be lost sight of, that Lodges are private organizations and privately maintained for their own members. There are some jurisdictions where it is not easy for visitors to gain admission and in these it becomes necessary to be specifically invited to attend a Lodge. And again, it must be remembered that every Mason has a right to prevent the visitation of any other Mason, not a member of his own Lodge to that Lodge—he need give no other reason therefore.

I have, for many years, devoted particular attention to colored Masonry and have read, correlated, and compiled all the available material, proceedings, Masonic histories, books and papers dealing with the subject from both the white and colored standpoint. In addition, I have corresponded with (and continue to do so) many colored brethren distinguished as Masons, and as students of Masonry, in their various Grand jurisdictions, and I am becoming more and more convinced that, the colored groups as separate and Grand bodies, are far better off and doing better work than if we had mixed lodges.

> I shall be very much interested in seeing the original work, a "Masonic Vade Mecum," commented on by Bro. Williamson, but I feel sure that no further remarks will be written by me, for I feel quite certain that Bro. Williamson has thoroughly done that job. No doubt I shall find lots to compliment Bro. Adams upon, and hence, I am risking nothing by congratulating him on a work which I feel sure has caused him many sleepless nights to compile—as a labor of love, no doubt.

An immediate reply by Bro. B.F. Adams in the next issue of The New York Age, to the strong criticisms by these two internationally recognized Masonic historians of his "Masonic Vade Mecum," was titled a "defense," yet, nearly one-half of the one thousand or more words used in his response, were devoted to the display of his fraternal and professional credentials. It would appear that Bro. Adams was less than responsive, not only to Voorhis' criticisms of earlier errors, but also to Williamson's more recent references to "big Masons," and the "book Masons, ritual parrots and emblem wearers" among the Craft. His "handful of hints" spread over nearly one hundred pages for the use of Craftsmen in Grand Lodge Schools of Instruction, presumed an ability to "read-between-the-lines" or as Williamson suggested, "remain in the dark, as far as the ideas are concerned, which the author had in mind at the time he wrote his brief."

Bro. B.F. Adams, Grand Lecturer of Missouri defended his "Masonic Vade Mecum." In the issues of The New York Age of July 20 and 27, appears a review by Bro. Harry A. Williamson:

> Noted New York Masonic student and historian, of no mean ability, of my booklet, the "Masonic Vade Mecum." Bro. Williamson has given the readers of The New York Age a careful and critical review, which I accept in the same friendly(?) and brotherly spirit that should ever prevail among Masons. However, the author, who is Grand Lecturer of Missouri, takes issue with Bro. Williamson in his analysis of several counts which he sets up for criticism, and on these counts, I shall set forth my contention for further review and criticism if any can be made.
>
> First, I want to compliment Bro. Williamson for the very high compliment which he pays me on my booklet. I assure him that I highly appreciate it and thank him. I am myself a Masonic student of many years hard study and Masonic research. I am an ex-teacher of forty years experience spent in the school room. I am also a member of the Philalethes Society—a society of Masons who make research and are prepared to write on the Philosophy of Ancient Craft Masonry. I am the only Negro, to my personal knowledge,

who holds a card of membership in this Society of 32nd and 33rd degree Masons. It is an international society with Hon. Alfred Moorhouse of Boston, Massachusetts, as president, and Cyrus F. Fields of Los Angeles, California, as secretary.

But further, I have been a constant reader of several leading journals and magazines on Freemasonry for years, and it was from The New York Age magazine, published in Washington, D.C., that I secured my information concerning the three mentioned in the "Masonic Vade Mecum."

And again in the matter of H.A.B. Solomon's great architect, I beg to advise that I know the story and life of that noted personage quite well, and even the history of his parentage, for of a truth, he was a half-Negro and half-Jew. But if Bro. Williamson could attend one of our Masonic Schools of Instruction, perhaps he would decide that I really "know my onions." And that I am somewhat acquainted with the story, history and legend of that wonderful personage, whom every regular Mason thinks so much of and who finally died a natural death AT HOME.

Again in the matter of the Master's hat, I did not intend, nor try to exhaust, this topic, nor tell every detail. I do this when in the School of Instruction. The hint in the "Masonic Vade Mecum," is only to make the brethren study and find out some things for themselves. However, in our regional Schools of Instruction, which are held periodically in fifteen districts in Missouri, these thinkings are fully explained. I simply hinted about the various titles by which Masonic jurisdictions are known. About half of the jurisdictions in the U.S. say AF&AM, while the other half say F&AM. However, there is no difference in meaning. All are regarded as regular.

Suffice it to say that the "Masonic Vade Mecum" was not intended to be sent out as an exhaustive treatise on the subjects contained in it; but rather as a handful of hints which were intended to arouse, inspire and cause the brethren of Missouri to begin to study, and make Masonic research to the end that, the work of our Masonic schools, might serve their aim and purpose to better advantage. And, too, that Masons might begin to find out the true and real meaning and the philosophy of Freemasonry, as practiced today. If this purpose can be served through a careful study of the "Masonic Vade Mecum," it will then have served its purpose and I, as its author, will have been compensated, even though I do not realize on the sale of this booklet as I had hoped.

In the matter of the "Scottish Rite" and "Symbolic Masonry," we need not get alarmed nor become confused in any manner. I know fully well that Ancient Craft Masonry, known today as Freemasonry, originally consisted of but three parts: degrees, together with the Holy Royal Arch, known as the Master's Part, and that our so-called higher degrees are all of more modern invention.

The Scottish Rite was worked out by the French and other European nations and the nobility, and brought to the United States long after Symbolic Masonry had been established, and was known throughout the United States. The author is a 32nd degree Mason by both the York and Scottish Rites and does not mix up Symbolic Masonry with this rite.

Again, Bro. Williamson brings me to task concerning my mention of the O.E.S. Why Bro. Williamson, even if England does not, almost the entire Masonic world recognizes this adoptive rite. Pennsylvania is the only grand jurisdiction of the United States which does not recognize and encourage the O.E.S., while every jurisdiction among our own race, as I understand, fully recognizes and encourages this adoptive rite, and they should do so. Don't you think so too, Bro. Williamson? Some form of adoptive rite has existed in Europe and Africa at least since the institution of our Ancient and Honorable Society, and my vision is that a greater future awaits our Adoptive bodies fraught with great opportunities and larger responsibilities. And to this I say: So may it be.

Finally, I repeat that I am very pleased with the critical review by Bro. Williamson of the "Masonic Vade Mecum," and wish it to be understood that his review has, by no means, aroused my ire, but that I am really proud to have a Masonic student and scholar critically review my booklet, and then recommend it so highly to the "higher ups" in Masonry, and especially to the Masonic Brotherhood universally.

The Grand Lodge of Missouri has approved the "Masonic Vade Mecum" and it is on sale in the office of the Grand Secretary, Dr. W.H. Mason of Marshall, Missouri.

Bro. Bertram L. Baker was addressed in "Masonic Notes" of The New York Age, August 31, 1935, as Bro. Williamson answers Bro. Adams:

The Masonic Editor, The New York Age, My Dear Brother:

Quite recently, you published a letter from Bro. B.F. Adams, Grand Lecturer of the Prince Hall Grand Jurisdiction of Missouri, commenting upon my review of the "Masonic Vade Mecum," a small pamphlet compiled by him and issued with the approval of the Grand Lodge. Bro. Adams considers my remarks "a careful and critical review...which I accept in the same friendly (?) and brotherly spirit which should ever prevail among Masons." If my remarks had been accepted in good faith, why has it been necessary for Bro. Adams to insert a "question mark" following the word "friendly"? From the tone of his comments upon several points brought forward, I am compelled to presume my review has been accepted in any but a friendly and brotherly spirit. I desire to assure Bro. Adams my remarks were written in all good faith; that a friendly criticism was directed only to such features in his volume as I deemed might require particular attention. I regret the intent of some of my remarks has been misinterpreted and since further comment has been solicited by him, I am accepting the suggestion.

I feel positive Bro. Adams thoroughly realizes that no two persons view the same thing in a similar light, consequently two writers will examine the same of a third from two other angles. I fully realize that in a volume of such character and size, it is impossible to discuss subjects in detail, but an author must appreciate the fact that the average reader can digest only what appears in the printed line, and except sufficient "light" is given a subject, the said average reader will still remain in the dark as far as the ideas are concerned, which the author had in mind at the time he wrote his brief.

a) The particular legendary individual so frequently referred to in our esoteric ceremonies. It is not my purpose to engage in a discussion relative to this person, but I still maintain a study of the researches on the subject as presented by J.S.M. Ward, one of England's best known Masonic scholars, would have been of both interest and value to Bro. Adams, and in addition to the volume mentioned in my review, I can recommend the three-volume set, "The Hung Society," by J.S.M. Ward and W.G. Stirling, London, 1925. Unfortunately, there are very few books extant upon this subject and the few that have been published are inaccessible to the average student.

b) The Master's Hat — about the Master's Hat. Did I criticize the reasons assigned by Bro. Adams for its use? Not at all. I merely added another suggestion, and while commenting upon this feature, I might suggest the Grand Lecturer examine the proceedings of the Grand Lodge of New York (Caucasian) for 1934, and on page 194, he will find some very interesting matters from the pen of Orian Long, Grand Historian, who in a footnote, says in part: "While originally a cleric — sacristan or monk — was the supervisor of Masons of the lodge, etc." Although this has particular reference to the "Vicar" or chaplain, it bears out my statement to the effect that such individuals, because of their higher education, must have presided over lodges during the earlier periods.

The historian of New York was discussing the customs in vogue about the year 1409. Accurate information upon this feature is meager, and the few volumes which might be of help are widely scattered and generally inaccessible. The little I have learned came from the files of the Builder (now defunct), formerly published at St. Louis, Missouri, by the late National Masonic Research Society.

c) As to the titles, "A.F. & A.M." and "F. & A.M." — among the Caucasians in the United States, their use invariably signifies from which of the English bodies they are descended, and in reality, have no other meaning. But if Bro. Adams will take time to examine the proceedings of each of those bodies, he will no doubt learn the greater portion use "A.F. & A.M." My opinion for the use of "F. & A.M." only by the Prince Hall group, has been represented in my review, therefore does not require repetition. I still maintain the reference in "Masonic Vade Mecum" is neither clear nor accurate.

d) Symbolic Masonry — Bro. Adams has misinterpreted my remarks relative to the use of the Scottish Rite numerals when discussing matters appertaining to Symbolic Masonry. To be frank, I consider such practices to be in very bad taste. The general public is not familiar with the line of demarcation between the Scottish and the so-called York Rite, and in that portion of readers, who become confused and imagine that a man, in order to be a "big Mason," or so-called "high Mason," must of necessity have added numerals following his name. During my career in the Fraternity, I have known any number of men who have started as Royal Arch, Templar, and Scottish Rite Masons, and then could not remember their oath and obligation as Symbolic Masons and could not function in a normal manner for all their "bigness."

It is not what the Grand Lecturer of Missouri knows about the differences between the two Rites, rather it is what the printed word conveys to the minds of the readers, and while I realize my own opinion upon this matter will not be acceptable to many, I still maintain it is in bad form for grand officers to place the said numerals after their names on Grand Lodge stationary. Bro. Adams states he is "a 32nd degree Mason by both the York and Scottish Rites." Does he really mean that? If so, since when has the former had more than the traditionary symbolic degrees, and how will Mr. Average Reader interpret the statement?

e) I am greatly surprised with Bro. Adams' statement relative to the Order of the Eastern Star. Does he desire the readers of The New York Age to gain the impression he does not understand the difference between that body and the Adoptive Lodges of Continental Europe of the 18th Century? If he can prove, through the presentation of indisputable evidence, that the two ever possessed intimate connection, or that the Star is descended from the Adoptive groups, I am willing to be convinced. The late Robert Morris, the founder of the Easter Star, at no time ever claimed his organization was in any legitimate manner connected with Symbolic Masonry. It is, like the American Doctrine of Exclusive Territorial Jurisdiction, purely an American invention, the only doubtful connection is the requirement that a Master Mason must serve in the station of Patron. The Adoptive Rite was of European origin and extent, and consisted of a group which was "adopted" by some lodge, just as the title implied. The male and female secret societies in Africa were entirely different, both in purpose and creation, than were the European Adoptive Lodges and the American Eastern Star. If Bro. Adams will study the origin and purpose of the African Societies, he will learn that such were in turn, exclusively for males, females, boys or girls, nor did they have any connection one with the other in any form.

J.S.M. Ward, in his volume, Freemasonry and the Ancient Gods, London, 1921, deals very extensively with the ancient secret societies in Asia, Africa, and Australia, and in none of his discussions does he indicate what Bro. Adams writes. Dudley Wright, in his book, Women and Freemasonry, London, 1922, fails to record any similarity between the Adoptive Lodge and the Eastern Star.

The O.E.S. — I still maintain that in a volume appertaining to Symbolic Masonry, any reference to the Star should have been omitted. The following is quoted from Bro. Adams' letter: "Why Bro. Williamson, even if England does not recognize this Adoptive Rite (O.E.S.), almost the entire Masonic World does; while Pennsylvania is the only Grand Jurisdiction of the U.S. that does not recognize and encourage the O.E.S." I can state without fear of contradiction that he is all wrong in such a statement. If he will examine the various proceedings of all the American bodies, he will learn of a considerable amount of legislation against the Star; he will find that in some states, it is forbidden to hold its meetings within the lodge rooms and temples. The organization is positively unknown outside of the United States, except in English speaking countries.

While on this subject, the following excerpt has been transcribed from the proceedings of the Grand Lodge of New York (Caucasian), for 1934, as found on pages 106-7, copies in part from the proceedings of the Grand Lodge of New Brunswick (Canada), for 1932.

A matter which caused him (Grand Master) serious concern was the Order of the Eastern Star, he holding that no brethren have any right to attend meetings of that organization and certainly should not become members thereof. He calls attention to action taken by the Grand Lodges of the British Empire, with regard to the matter. He urges that the Craft in New Brunswick place itself on record as disapproving of any brothers joining that organization or having anything to do with it; the lodge should have their undivided allegiance.

The Grand Lodge evidently agreed fully with the Grand Master in this matter. A resolution embodying recommendations of the Grand Master was adopted "with much applause."

From the same volume of proceedings, the Fraternal correspondent of New York has transcribed the following from the same Canadian body, and as found in the proceedings for 1933:

In a Special Committee Report concerning the Eastern Star, several concise definitions were submitted. One is that the Order is not and cannot be affiliated and connected with Masonry in any respect. Secretaries of Lodges are warned that it is unlawful to give to anyone, to use in connection with the Order, any information regarding the standing of the members in the Lodges. Suggested is that Grand Lodge is not warranted to approve the Order, which in some instances may prove harmful to the peace and harmony of local groups of Masons. The report closes by recommending that the Order should be allowed to pursue its own course in the same manner as any other Order composed entirely of women, but the Grand Lodge cannot countenance even an appearance of a connection between Masonry and the Eastern Star.

Some years following the invasion of the Eastern Star, the subject was brought to the attention of the Grand Lodge of England and it forbade its members serving in the office of Patron in any Chapter formed within its territory. In order to overcome this situation, brethren who belong to lodges under the Grand Lodge of Scotland and who resided in England replaced this practice. The reason Pennsylvania interdicted its members with the Eastern Star was because the women had so meddled into Masonic affairs, even to the point of approving or disapproving candidates for membership in lodges, or for election to office in both lodges and the Grand Lodge itself. In New York, the matter of the women has been of no small amount of discussion in Grand Lodge. It appears that for many years, there has been a controversy for control of the Star between the Catholic and Protestant wives of Freemasons.

f) Separation is Best — This lengthy discussion of the Eastern Star really has no place in this communication and, but for Bro. Adams' comment, would not have been introduced. In my opinion, the Star is an excellent organization, it has been of great service to the women and has been of great help in the maintenance of homes for both men and women. While it has been of great assistance in some instances, it has caused friction in Craft circles.

If I recall correctly, our brethren in Missouri have experienced considerable trouble and I believe it was due to the fact its Grand Lodge attempted to control the Order in that state, although I admit, I am not conversant with the facts. In our own jurisdiction in New York, brethren whose wives have been or who still may be in the Order, attempted on several occasions to dabble into the business of the women.

My advice is, take the men out of the Star and permit the women to manage their own business.

There is much agreement among Prince Hall Craftsmen that some sort of manual or "vade mecum" ought to be made available through Grand Lodge and subordinate lodge Schools of Instruction, not only for some common understanding of the philosophy and practices of Freemasonry, but also to address many of the myths and misconceptions too often circulated by well meaning members of the Fraternity. These discussions between outstanding scholars, held even fifty years ago, provide both the <u>essential</u> <u>cautions</u> and the <u>appropriate</u> <u>models</u> that are to be observed by contemporary Freemasons who may be bold enough to attempt to swim in these largely uncharted seas; providing public information about the Craft.

Brother Harry A. Williamson spent the largest portion of his lifetime in research and investigation, and the dissemination of his findings about Freemasonry in general and about Prince Hall Masonry in particular. His published works include: The Prince Hall Primer, A Brief History of Negro Masonry, Freemasonry in West Virginia, Prince Hall Masonry in New York State, A Chronological History of Prince Hall Masonry, along with many newspaper and magazine articles.

This paper is one attempt to bring to light the work of this internationally acknowledged Masonic scholar, which has, for too many years, been unavailable to members of our Craft. His discussion about the legendary figures in Masonry, details such as the Master's hat, the use of letters (A.F. & A.M. and F. & A.M.), the relationship between symbolic Masonry and Scottish Rite Masonry, and the proper role and function of the Order of the Eastern Star; even during such a review of Bro. B.F. Adams' booklet (also unavailable), point the direction for present day writers who try to follow in his foot steps.

COMMENTS

Reverend Robert L. Uzzel, F.P.S. writes:

I wish to thank Bro. Bass for an outstanding and enjoyable paper. The only real criticism I have is that I had some difficulty at times determining when Bro. Bass was speaking and when Bro. Williamson was speaking.

I would like to comment on some of Williamson's points. Having been raised in the Caucasian Grand Lodge of Texas, A.F. & A.M., I have never really been able to understand all the concern over the F. & A.M./A.F. & A.M. question. On page 31, of Williamson's Prince Hall Primer, he stated: "As of July 1, 1956, only one Grand Lodge used the word 'Ancient' in its corporate title, and that is Virginia." I understand that since then, Virginia has dropped the "Ancient" from its name. Williamson further stated, in response to the question, "Why has the word 'Ancient' been discontinued? " That it has been, "Because it is absolutely without significance to Freemasons of color." Personally, I believe that Black Masons have as much claim as White Masons to antiquity. Although modern speculative Masonry goes back only to the 18th century, Masonic legends are quite ancient in origin. The craft has drawn its symbolism from a variety of ancient sources. I recognize that the term "three-letter" as opposed to "four-letter," for us as Prince Hall Freemasons, serves a practical purpose to distinguish us from Grand Lodges such as the one to which I formerly owed allegiance, and from unrecognized Black Masons; yet, I feel much too much has been made over this matter. If today, a Prince Hall Grand Lodge desired to call itself "Ancient Free and Accepted," there would be nothing wrong with it. That is my opinion.

Williamson mentioned a lodge in Africa open only to men with annual incomes in excess of $40,000.00. If this lodge was never declared "clandestine," it should have been — and by all legitimate Grand Lodges. In the degree of Entered Apprentice, we are taught that Freemasonry regards no man for his worldly wealth or possessions, and that it is the internal and not the external qualifications which qualify a man for Masonry. This lodge is an insult to Masonic ideals. I have elsewhere expressed my belief that Masonic fees, especially in the "higher degrees," and in the Shrine, are far too high in many places. I am not comfortable with the reputation of a "middle class organization," and am repelled by the idea of an aristocratic group.

Included is an interesting discussion of Alpha Lodge No. 116 of Newark (now East Orange), New Jersey, an all-black lodge under the jurisdiction of the Caucasian Grand Lodge of New Jersey. I do not agree with Bro. Walkes' contention that there is no need for Alpha Lodge as long as there is a Prince Hall Grand Lodge of New Jersey. The statement is made by Williamson, "so far as the members are concerned, their Masonic activity consists of going to their own Lodge (with rare exceptions), attending Grand Lodge of Instruction once a year, and Grand Lodge once a year." This seems to indicate that they do not visit White lodges in New Jersey nor do they belong to, or participate in, Scottish or York Rites. Walkes has previously reported about a Past Master of Alpha Lodge being blackballed when he applied for membership in a Royal Arch Chapter. I have considered writing to Salaam Temple, A.A.O.N.M.S. in Newark, New Jersey, to ask if any Alpha Lodge brother has ever been a member of this temple. If I did, however, I doubt if I would receive a reply, since they regard me as "clandestine."

Perhaps Hiram Abiff was half-Jewish and half-Black. Maybe; maybe not. It makes no difference. No Mason who has studied the Bible and Masonic history takes seriously the claim of assassination by three "ruffians." That, of course, is a legend used to teach a moral lesson. Masonry is full of myths, and myths are not the same as lies. All civilizations have their myths and myths serve their purposes, some more legitimate than others.

Bro. Williamson was correct in taking Bro. Adams to task for calling himself "a 32nd degree Mason by both the York and Scottish Rites." The York Rite does not have that many degrees. However, I regret that, currently, being a Knight Templar does not carry the honor that being a 32nd degree Scottish Rite Mason does. The main thing the two have in common is that they are both doors to the Mystic Shrine.

The discussion of the Order of the Eastern Star also deserves comment. This is certainly not a Masonic organization as no woman can be a Mason. It is primarily a woman's order, although some men belong. I find it strange to find Masons who are members of both the Eastern Star and the Heroines of Jericho, whose wives are in neither society. I do not belong to either adoptive body and doubt that I ever will.

I recall an incident about ten years ago when I was in the White Masons, and was invited to join a White Eastern Star Chapter. I told the District Deputy that I had little interest in the Eastern Star and, being single at the time, saw no value in joining. He replied that there were single women in the Eastern Star. I then terminated the conversation as I could not bring myself to reveal that I was not interested in White women. I certainly have more positive feelings toward the Prince Hall Eastern Star. The fact that many Prince Hall Freemasons have been confused about the proper roles of the Eastern Star, however, can be seen at the offense taken by one Grand Master to words written by the late Grand Master John G. Lewis, Jr., of Louisiana in The Phylaxis, 4th Quarter, 1978, pp. 42-3:

Another concern in which the roots of dissension are found is that of the legisla-

> tion pertaining to female bodies to the effect that a female must join the Order of the Eastern Star before joining any other female order.
>
> There is no progression or succession in the female orders. Their membership is not predicated each upon the other. This is also true of their ritualistic work. Each is entirely independent and without reference to the other.
>
> There can be found no responsible authority which equates the Order of the Eastern Star with the Symbolic Lodge. The Order of the Eastern Star is adopted by a Grand Lodge as an auxiliary and not a counterpart or equal. The same is true of the other female bodies.
>
> Each may be adopted as auxiliaries to the recognized and affiliated bodies. Certainly, a Grand Lodge can pass such a regulation in the sense that it can and will do anything it wishes, but such a regulation does not have the sanction of law or custom and its enactment is the assertion of an arbitrary will.

The Eastern Star has no doubt rendered much service to the craft. But it is no more Masonic than any of our other adoptive bodies. I was disappointed that the charter of the Phyllis Chapter requires Eastern Star membership as a prerequisite. I feel that membership should be open to members of any adoptive body, including the Daughters of Isis, to which my wife belongs.

There is a discussion of the negative attitude of English Masons toward the Eastern Star. This could possibly be related to the presence in England of the unrecognized body known a Co-Masonry which admits both men and women. At one time, one of the leaders of English Co-Masonry was Rt. Rev. Sir Hugh Sykes, presiding bishop of the Liberal Catholic Church, a blend of Catholicism and Theosophy. Co-Masonry is a good topic for future research.

Also mentioned are African secret societies. A number of writers have correctly observed that at no time have Black Americans organized facsimiles of African secret societies. What, if anything, such African orders have in common with Freemasonry is a topic worth exploring. Currently, I do not know enough about this subject to express an opinion.

Hopefully, one day Adams' booklet and Williamson's out-of-print works will be reprinted for the benefit of the craft. Bro. Bass' evaluation of Williamson is right on key. In discussing Voorhis, however, he fails to mention the very significant fact that, in later years, Voorhis became a turncoat and a bitter enemy of Prince Hall Freemasonry. Any reading of Voorhis should take this into consideration.

Thanks again to Bro. Bass for a unique contribution to Prince Hall Masonic literature.

Joseph A. Walkes , Jr. F.P.S., writes:

I want to thank Bro. Bass for this extraordinarily interesting paper. Bro. Bass continues to put together well researched works. This paper is of particular interest to me because it deals with three Freemasons whose writings have either come to my notice, as in the case of Bro. Adams, or who have been meaningful to my Masonic education such as Bro. Williamson, or have earned my utter contempt as in the case of turncoat Harold Van Buren Voorhis.

Bro. Professor B.F. Adams was a member of my Prince Hall Grand Lodge of Missouri and therefore because of Bro. Bass' paper, I have been able to research some of his writings, and to learn something about him. What follows I hope will add to Bro. Bass' paper.

Professor B.F. Adams was a member of Golden Gate Lodge No. 115, Springfield, Missouri, having been a member before 1890. He was elected Grand Lecturer, Southern District by unanimous vote, August 12, 1922, at the 56th Annual Session of the Grand Lodge held in St. Louis.[1] At the time, the Missouri Jurisdiction had two Grand Lecturers, Northern and Southern Districts.

In giving his report of the first year of his stewardship, Adams reported that he had visited 75 lodges, written 400 letters, and 100 postcards, and held "schools of instructions" in each Lodge visited:

> How well I have succeeded in giving new light and visions of the real spirit and teachings in the philosophy and symbolism of Speculative Masonry, is left to the brethren of the Lodges who heard me talk, and who witnessed my explanation of the symbolism.[2]

Bro. Adams immediately set out to make major changes in the operation of the Craft. First, he leveled criticism of the teachings of the past:

> ...my observations are that the rank and file of the Brotherhood have not had the real essence and spirit of Freemasonry, due, no doubt, to the practice, teaching and traditions of the "Fathers" of the Craft, who were inclined to the imperfect teach-

> ings of our early Masonic brethren, who were not so erudite in the principles and correct practices of our ancient and honored fraternity.
>
> However, I do not lay this fault to those who in later years preceded me, as teachers of Masonic practices. Hence, I present no criticism, even upon our "Fathers" who first taught the Craft. They did and taught what they knew; they taught as they had been taught, and...so we say: "He who does his best, does well."[3]

With that, Bro. Adams made his role clear to the Jurisdiction, and perhaps it was his belief in this role that lead to his writing his "Masonic Vade Mecum" and his other writings:

> The office of Grand Lecturer has never had the rightful consideration given it by our group of Masons in former years. The office was looked upon simply in name and the officer functioning only now and then, sometimes not at all. This was a mistake and proved a detriment to the brotherhood. Dr. Mackey says that the Grand Lecturer is the most important office of the Grand Lodge and that he is the acknowledged Masonic teacher, and he should be more than a mere ritualist. He should know Masonic History, the writings of eminent and distinguished Masonic writers and scholars, with a knowledge of the Bible, that he may be able to teach Masonry and explain its symbolism.[4]

In his 1924 report to the Grand Lodge, he presented three recommendations that are most interesting:

1) That the barbaric practice now used in the 3rd Degree ceremonies which I am not permitted to enlarge on in writing, be abandoned, as un-Masonic, and in many instances dangerous and hurtful, and that this law become effective on the rise of this Session.

2) That every subordinate lodge hereafter be required to use for the initiation of candidates, "Duncan's Revised and Complete Ritual," which will make the work of initiation uniform, and in keeping with Masonic progress.

3) That every lodge abandon the unsanitary and un-Masonic use of the "Pastos," a relic of barbarism and really uncalled for in the ceremonies of the 3rd Degree.[5]

I am sure that all of the readers of Lux e Tenebris understand exactly what Bro. Adams alluded to in his first recommendation. However, his second recommendation is rather important, for today in 1985, unfortunately, the Prince Hall Grand Lodge continues to use this so-called "Duncan's Revised Ritual." It is unfortunate because it is profusely illustrated, which means that it must be kept under lock and key; and second, it is an "expose" printed by Ezra A. Cook Publications of Chicago, Illinois, a publishing house established in 1867 by Mr. Cook, who was "unalterably opposed to secret orders."

Bro. Adams' third recommendation gives us a glimpse as to the practices being used in the Lodges at the time, by the mention of "Pastos," a Greek word meaning "a couch." The Pastos, being a chest or close cell, in the Pagan mysteries, among the Druids, an excavated stone, in which the aspirant was for some time placed, to commemorate the mystical death of the god. This constituted the symbolic death which was common to all the mysteries. Bro. Adams' usage however, is "coffin."

Bro. Bass notes that in the October issue of The Square & Compass (Denver, Colorado), for 1934, there appeared an article by Bro. Adams. I thought it would be of interest to publish that article and Voorhis' response to it:

FREEMASONRY AS PRACTICED AMONG COLORED MEN NOT CLANDESTINE

By B.F. Adams, 32°, Grand Lecturer of Colored Masons
for Missouri and Her Masonic Jurisdiction

The question is frequently asked: Are colored Masons regular, or are they clandestine? To answer this very pertinent and important question, one must know the record of Freemasonry in America, and especially in the United States. Also when and how it was established and by what authority. Again, to properly answer this question those who attempt to answer it must first rid themselves of any and all feelings of race prejudice and political self bias.

They must be fully possessed with the immutable principles and teachings as is set forth in that tenet of Freemasonry which declares: That by practice of brotherly love, we are taught to regard the whole human species as one common family, created by one Almighty Parent. The high, the low, the rich and poor, inhabitants of the same planet, are to aid, protect and support each other. On this principle, Masonry unites men of every country, sect and opinion, and conciliates true friendship among those who might otherwise have remained at a perpetual distance.

If this question is answered in keeping with this declaration, and is devoid of race prejudice, the answer will be yes, Freemasonry as practiced among the colored men is regular, and by no means clandestine, since the Grand Lodge of England, which chartered our Lodges of white brethren in America, is the same Grand Lodge that chartered and authorized colored men to practice Freemasonry in America.

So the records will show that, because of race prejudice, and previous conditions of the black man in the United States, many of the Grand Lodges (white) have barred colored men and set up the claim that they were clandestine, because they have followed in the wake of our white brethren in establishing what they are pleased to call "American Independence in Masonic Jurisdiction," which means that the American Lodges declared themselves free and independent of English control or jurisdiction.

Again, since Freemasonry teaches the Fatherhood of God and the Brotherhood of Man, and both white and black received their degrees from the same fountainhead—the Grand Lodge of England—and our white brethren were finally declared as rebels against their government, and by the revolution virtually lost their Masonic standing, while the colored brethren simply declared themselves free from English rule and jurisdiction in the light of real facts and proof, who, if either, should be called or spoken of as being clandestine, the colored Masons or our white brethren?

Will some brother who knows the record answer this question, without a thought or feeling that is tinged with race prejudice or hatred? But now let the record in this matter speak: The Grand Lodge of Massachusetts led the way in the American Revolution, as she also did in the matter of American Doctrine of Grand Lodge Jurisdiction, thus severing herself from all Masonic allegiance to England, the Mother Grand Lodge. The other didn't give Massachusetts' Grand Lodge any right whatever to take this action, and as African Lodge No. 459 followed in the wake of our white brethren in making such a declaration, that is, in 1827, when Prince Hall Grand Lodge of Massachusetts declared herself independent of the Grand Lodge of England, and set up for herself in America, did she by this action become any more clandestine than did our white brethren whom she followed in this action? This is the record, who will dispute it?

But further, if Freemasonry as practiced among colored men is clandestine, then why do our white brethren recognize and fellowship the Masons of the Republic of Haiti, who are all colored men and whose Grand Lodge is in our calendar of Grand Lodges. These Negro Masons are accepted by the entire Masonic world as regular, and further, the Republic of Liberia, with its Grand Lodge of Negro Masons, is also recognized as regular, but more yet:

Alpha Lodge No. 116 of Newark, New Jersey, all colored men, is under the direct control of the Grand Lodge (white) of the Commonwealth of New Jersey, while Thistle Lodge No. 1003, of Panama (Isthmus), is under the control of the Grand Lodge of Scotland. Also, Union Lodge No. 18 of Halifax, N.S., all colored men, is under the direct control of the Grand Lodge of England. And all of these Lodges are composed of colored brethren. No Grand Lodge that we know of thinks of them as clandestine Masons, but they are recognized as regular and are fellowshipped as Free and Accepted Masons throughout the Masonic world. Then what is the matter in America? The land of the free and the home of the brave; the land where our fathers died; the land where Freemasonry has contributed so much in making it the pride of all of her citizens?

Let us have more of the record: Sibley, in his story of Freemasonry, says: Race prejudice exists to some extent among Freemasons, although properly it has, or can have, no place in so cosmopolitan an institution. And while it has not barred any race from Freemasonry, it has denied recognition in some localities to the Negro race, and to individual Masons of the Hebraic division of the Semitic race. Dr. Mackey says: Recognition and legality are two very distinct questions. Legality of Freemasonry among the colored race cannot be questioned, since it came from the same source as did the practice among white Masons, but the question of recognition in America is based upon the principle of American Independence of Grand Lodge Jurisdiction. This was established just before the institution of African Lodge No. 459, and has been followed by a majority of the Grand Lodges (white) of America.

The Grand Lodge of Washington, in 1897, said:

> Resolved, that in the opinion of this Grand Lodge, Masonry is universal, and without doubt, neither race nor color are among the tests proper to be applied to determine the fitness of a candidate for the degrees of Masonry.
>
> Resolved, further, that in view of the recognized laws of the Masonic institution and of facts of history authenticated and worthy of credence, this Grand Lodge does not see its way clear to deny or question the right of its Lodges or members thereof, to recognize as brother Masons, Negroes who have been initiated in Lodges which can trace their origin to Prince Hall Lodge no. 459, organized under the warrant of our R.W. Brother Thos. Howard, Earl of Effingham, etc., bearing date of Sept. 29, A.L. 5784, and to our Worthy Brother

Prince Hall, W.M., of African Lodge No. 459."

> This opinion made no little stir among a number of Grand Lodges in the United States. However, they have restored friendly relations with Washington again and so, as Sibley says: "Prejudice exists to some extent, although it has no place in the great body of Masons, for the Negro is not clandestine in his practice of Freemasonry. If there is any regular practice in America the Negro must ever share this regularity." "Convin cam sine gas."

At first blush, Bro. Adams published an interesting article, especially in my view of the fact that it was being carried in a Caucasian Masonic publication, whose readership was primarily white. Harold V.B. Voorhis responded in the January, 1935, issue of the same publication. At the time, Voorhis was a continuing student of Masonry, and had maintained close ties with Bro. Williamson and Prince Hall Freemasonry, both of which he supported. However, forty-seven years later, he would earn the contempt of this writer and other knowledgeable Masonic scholars by his turncoat anti-Prince Hall stance. After a half a century of assisting Prince Hall Freemasonry, Voorhis would turn his back on Black America and would begin writing anti-Prince Hall articles to include his naive foreword from the infamous book, <u>A Documentary Account of Prince Hall and Other Black Fraternal Orders</u>, by Henry Wilson Coil, Sr. and John MacDuffie Sherman, Editor; two men whose hostility towards Prince Hall Freemasonry are well known. In his foreword, Voorhis would write that the segregation within American Freemasonry had nothing to do with racism but was the fault of "the segregation of colored men themselves from the organization which was started by white men."

Voorhis responded to Bro. Adams under title of "Negro Masonry-Again," and noted that Prince Hall Freemasonry could not be classed as Clandestine.

> It is perfectly obvious from the line of thought introduced into this article, just what the writer is trying to prove. While the logic may be good and the legal and moral aspects may be correct in themselves, no amount of reasoning can rearrange a condition existing since the very beginning of Freemasonry in the United States.
>
> There is no question of hatred involved in the situation at all. Most writers on this subject forget that a Masonic lodge is made up of a group of men who are for the most part, social friends. They receive into their group those citizens they desire—under a code of rules or laws they have made for themselves for their own government, commensurate with Masonic usage. If these Lodges form a Grand Lodge among themselves, this does not affect the position of the individual lodges.

They have an inherent right to accept those they desire into their own lodges. So far, I have never discovered a law actually prohibiting colored members in an American Lodge. On the contrary, I have, in my files, numerous examples of colored brethren having been made Masons in white lodges and of colored brethren as members of such lodges.

Regardless of the technical discussion surrounding the formation of Grand Lodges or the Grand Lodge in Massachusetts, which is the one usually taken into consideration by writers on the position of the negro or colored Mason, we are faced with a condition of existence that has been in operation for nearly a hundred and fifty years. This cannot be overcome by any legal argument, as already stated. Continued recognition of these many years of, for example, the Grand Lodge of Massachusetts, places the stamp of approval on these bodies and their actions which might, under different circumstances, be open to question. Then too, we have the additional fact that the Grand Lodge of England, and those Grand Lodges of other English speaking countries, all recognize Massachusetts and our other Grand Lodges as regular.

As to which lodges are clandestine and which are irregular, there can be little discussion. No one familiar with the proper meaning of the two terms, and history of the development of colored Masonry in the United States, can consider the colored lodges as clandestine—only irregular, since they have not been rechartered by the present Grand Lodges.

This condition is reciprocal, if need be. No question of clandestinism enters into the subject at all. A clandestine body is one that is set up without any authority whatever, i.e., by expelled Masons or by men that may never have received the degrees at all, except through some illegitimate channel. While it may not be recognized with Masonic regulations, or what not, there can be no question of their derivation, i.e., the Grand Lodge of England, and hence, they cannot be clandestine.

So far as the illustrations of negro lodges given in the article in question are concerned, two are outside of the U.S. and have no concern in this discussion. The other (Alpha, No. 116 of New Jersey, in which I have sat) may be mentioned in truthfulness as the writer has done, but so far as the members are concerned, their Masonic activity consists of going to their own Lodge (with rare exceptions), attending Grand Lodge of Instruction and Grand Lodge once a year (officers).

One of them, No. 18, is not in existence. In 1855, five colored men were initiated in Royal Sussex Lodge, No. 6, R.S.N. They subsequently applied to the Hon. Alexander Keith, the District Grand Lodge of England in Nova Scotia, for a dispensation. This was granted and a charter was issued on December 3, 1856, by the Grand Lodge of England, No. 994. The number was changed in 1863 to 693. The Lodge joined the Grand Lodge of Nova Scotia in 1869, and was assigned the number 18. The Lodge did good work for many years when it was in the hands of capable brethren, and they confined their candidates to men of color; but about 1910, they accepted petitions from any man of color, no matter where he resided, whether in Nova Scotia, British Columbia, and occasionally, from the United States.

The secretary became short in his accounts and the records and minutes were not properly kept, with the result that, after investigation, the Grand Lodge took up the Charter in June, 1916, and the Lodge has not functioned since. The members in good standing were given demits at large. One or two of the brethren affiliated with other Lodges but it is difficult for them to get in.

The thought must not be lost sight of, that Lodges are private organizations and privately maintained for their own members. There are some jurisdictions where it is not easy for visitors to gain admission and in these it becomes necessary to be specifically invited to attend a lodge. And again, it must be remembered that every Mason has a right to prevent the visitation of any other Mason not a member of his own lodge to that lodge—and he need give no reason therefore.

I have, for many years, devoted particular attention to colored Masonry and have read, correlated and compiled all available material, written material, proceedings, Masonic histories, books and papers from both white and colored standpoints. In addition, I have corresponded (and continue to) with many colored brethren distinguished as Masons, and students of Masonry in their various bodies and Grand bodies, and I am becoming more and more convinced that the colored groups as separate Grand and subordinate bodies, are far better off and doing better work than if we had "mixed" lodges.

May I leave this thought for our colored brethren to consider: Before bothering about recognition or what not from Caucasian Grand bodies—get your own house in order. There is hardly a state in the Union where there are not two or more Grand bodies of colored Masons working. Our correspondent may not realize this condition of brethren because Missouri is one of the few jurisdictions of colored Masons who started as a Prince Hall group (December 20, 1866), and has continued so, without interruption nor invasion by other groups. They have had a regular succession of Grand Masters (serving an average of three to four years—except J.H. Pelham who served sixteen years) and have, therefore, had more success than most of their sister jurisdictions, who have not been so well off.

May I further point out (and I have seen the original Warrant of African Lodge No. 459) that the warrant granted by the Grand Lodge of England to Prince Hall in 1784, does not provide for the making of Masons—a fact which seems to have been overlooked by many writers on the technical side of this interesting subject.

As can be seen from the Voorhis answer to Bro. Adams' article, that even then he was a propagandist and an apologist for regular Freemasonry. His statement that he had never heard of legislation passed by white Grand Lodges against the initiation of Blacks into the Lodges under their jurisdiction, smacks either of pure ignorance or pure hyperbole.

It is also interesting to note that Voorhis, himself a member of the Caucasian Grand Lodge of New Jersey, explains that Alpha Lodge No. 116 (which has no reason for being in existence, for it is a token Lodge), does not or cannot participate in the affairs of its white "plantation" Masters, the so-called regular Freemasonry. In a word, they do not visit other white Lodges where they are not wanted, do not petition for higher degrees such as the Scottish Rite where they are also not wanted, and are quite happy in their "house-nigger" existence.

Once again, I want to thank Bro. Bass for a most interesting paper and I know that my fellow Lux e Tenebris members will find it interesting and educational.

NOTES

[1] Proceedings of the Prince Hall Grand Lodge of Missouri (henceforth called Proceedings), 1923, page 107.

[2] Proceedings, 1923, p. 104.

[3] Ibid, p. 104.

[4] Proceedings, 1924, p. 107.

[5] Ibid, p. 109

Brian L. Abrams, Sr., M.P.S. writes:

Since being introduced to the writings of the late Bro. Harry Williamson, I have developed a great appreciation for his usually thorough researches. Bro. Harold Van Buren Voorhis, like the late General Albert Pike, has made many contributions to Masonic writings, and since 1963, has developed the same attitude as did Bro. Pike when it concerns Prince Hall Masonry.

I congratulate Bro. Bass on his re-introduction of a very interesting concept to disperse Masonic light. I am uncertain as to the total content, but I understand that the M.W. Grand Lodge of Indiana (Prince Hall Grand Lodge of Indiana) has quite a comprehensive manual of procedures, etc. The concept of a Prince Hall Freemasonry Handbook makes one wonder how the hurdles of the various jurisdictional customs and traditions will be overcome? Bro. Bass, I would like to know if a photocopy of the "Masonic Vade Mecum," by Bro. Adams, is available? In regard to the debate of the Master's Hat, I have enclosed a photocopy of page 179 of "A History of Freemasonry," that mentions a universal history by a Benedictine Monk, that was thought to be a reference for the "Matthew Cook MS,"which lends itself to the statements made by Bro. Williamson on page 13, paragraph (B).

The answer to the question of a need for a Prince Hall Masonic Handbook is partially answered in the first paragraph of the Editorial of the July 1985, Vol. 1 Newsletter of The Phylaxis Society. Thank you Bro. Bass for the opportunity to learn of another Masonic effort by a Prince Hall Mason.

Robert L. Cannady writes:

Bro. or Dr. Floyd Bass has done a tremendous piece of literature in the writing of DO PRINCE HALL MASONS NEED A HANDBOOK OF FREEMASONRY? I would go so far as to say it is a masterpiece of writing.

Figuratively speaking, one can clearly see that Bro. Bass has really done his homework in writing on "A MASONIC VADE MECUM, or manual."

Bro. Bass takes us back fifty years to a controversial article that appeared in Bertram L. Baker's "Masonic Notes," in The New York Age. This particular article refers to Bro. B.F. Adam's booklet containing about 92 pages, and the gist of what the Brother was trying to put into effect, was a manual for the Grand Lodge School of Instruction for his jurisdiction.

It seems that Bro. Adams made a few errors in his manual or book, and was criticized by both late great Masonic Historians, Harry A. Williamson and Voorhis. I am sorry that Bro. Williamson and Bro. Adams could not have necessarily gotten their heads together on this matter, as for the later Voorhis, not taking anything away from him, because he, Voorhis, was a great "Bigot" too. As the saying goes, "to err is human," therefore, Bro. Adams did the same thing that most of us do sometime in our lives, he made a few errors in his booklet. I guess both men, being the great historians or lecturers they were, just could not get their heads together.

Just what did this booklet contain? As Bro. Bass says, the first chapter carries about 13 subdivisions under appropriate titles. Bro. Adams outlines Speculative Masonry and references are made to moral and religious doctrines and beliefs in (G.A.O.U.). Also, the "Higher Degrees" is mentioned, but we all know that there are only 3 degrees including the H.R.A.D. Bro. Bass explains that he is just trying to give an explanation of some of the beauty in the concordant bodies.

Secondly, Bro. Adams gives a list of Biblical references and their connection with our Fraternity.

Thirdly, a brief reference to the origin of the jurisdiction of Missouri is also mentioned, and Bro. Adams generalizes about a certain authority in reference to the above, but fails to give the author's name and title of his work, probably assuming or taking for granted that the reader knows who this authority is.

Fourth, Bro. Adams asks why does the W.M. wear a hat, and gives three reasons for the same; while Bro. Bass mentions several logical reasons for the W.M. wearing a hat too.

Fifth, Bro. Adams talks about the ritual and the symbols appertaining to the E.A. and F.C. Degrees, plus the twelve original points and what one can obtain from membership in the Craft.

In Chapter II, Bro. Adams tries to explain about the rights and powers of a Lodge and the reason for the apron. Bro. Adams does his best to explain about the use of "A.F. & A.M." in some of our American Jurisdictions as used by Black and White "Masons," even though he does not make himself quite clear.

Chapter III, as Bro. Bass says, is devoted to ritualistic questions and answers. Under the "Masonic Notes of Interest," Bro. Adams quotes from "The Northern Freemason" (English), in reference to natives being denied admission as members or visitors in Lodges in Africa. I concur with Bro. Bass on that situation, because I have friends in Ghana and Nigeria whom belong to mixed Lodges. I hate to make the statement, but the U.S.A. is the main perpetrator in relation to that situation other than South Africa. I personally met brothers in Ghana and Nigeria at Howard University that were teaching my sons, whom are also members of the Craft and belong to mixed Lodges in Africa, the mother country.

In Chapter IV, Bro. Adams goes into the historical aspect of certain ceremonies and also tries to relate ancient Hebrew history to the Craft. He devotes a small segment to "H.A.B.," and talks about making Freemasons "at sight."

The Good Bro. Bass gives a thumbnail sketch of Chapter V, which deals with the poetic and religious side of Freemasonry, Knights, Templars, Landmarks, etc.

In Chapter VI, Bro. Adams deals with the regularity of Black Masonry. I concur with Bro. Bass when he says, that the author should refrain from using the numeral (32°) when writing about the subject of Ancient Craft Masonry, because, as I mentioned earlier, just the same as Bro. Bass stated, there are only three degrees (3) including the "H.R.A. Degree." Bro. Bass goes on to say that Bro. Adams does not mention why Alpha No. 116, Thistle No. 1013, and Union No. 18, are not considered as "Clandestine" by certain jurisdictions throughout the world. The reason is simple, because this is the U.S.A., and they were formed by White Jurisdictions, as simple as that. As for the Mother Grand Lodge in Boston, of all Prince Hall Masons, if I recollect, it is the only Lodge that has its original "Charter" from England. I could question about how certain jurisdictions came about their Charter, but this is not the time or place.

In this chapter, Bro. Adams also talks about the Order of the Eastern Stars. I am again in accord with Bro. Bass in relation to this situation. Why would he want to bring the Stars into his booklet? They are separate organizations, and have nothing whatsoever to do with Masonry. I realize that many of our wives are members of that particular organization and the Order has done a great many beneficial things for the Craft, but it is still not a part of the Craft. In several Caucasian American Jurisdictions, the O.E.S. is forbidden to meet in Masonic Temples, and some jurisdictions do not even allow members of the Craft to belong to that order.

Other than that exception, I think Bro. Adams has put together a great booklet and other jurisdictions should take heed to it and try and get their Grand Jurisdictions to put something together similar to Bro. Adams booklet.

As for commenting on the late Harold Van Buren Voorhis' remarks, I will make them very short, because I have very little patience for a "Bigot" of his kind, and I quote:

> I have, for many years, devoted particular attention to colored Masonry and have read, correlated and compiled all the available proceedings, Masonic histories, books, and papers dealing with the subject from both the white and colored standpoint. In addition, I have corresponded with (and continue to do so) many colored brethren distinguished as Masons and as students of Masonry in their various Grand jurisdictions, and I am becoming more and more convinced that the colored groups as "separate Grand Bodies" are far better off and doing better than if we had mixed Lodges."

From the above quote, I became very annoyed and found myself thinking negatively too.

Bro. Adams, defended his "Vade Mecum" in the July 20 and 27 issues of 1935, of The New York Age. He, therefore, went into a long dissertation explaining why the booklet was written and the purpose of it. He also elaborated on A.F. & A.M., the "Scottish Rite" and "Symbolic Masonry."

Bro. Adams defended, or tried to explain his remarks in reference to the O.E.S. in his rebuttal to Bro. Williamson's remarks, in Bro. Bertram L. Baker's column.

Lengthy discussions went on between these two heavy Brothers which could have been put to use in putting Prince Hall Masonry in the forefront of all other jurisdictions.

In conclusion, I wish to say that Bro. Bass has done a very good job in analyzing "A Masonic Vade Mecum," and has brought back into light, again, a piece of literature that perhaps a lot of us Brothers would not have known about, had it not been for his masterpiece of writing on the subject. Keep up the good work, Bro. Bass.

www.ingramcontent.com/pod-product-compliance
Lightning Source LLC
Chambersburg PA
CBHW081141300726
48982CB00006B/1033